❖ Dedication ❖

To my mom and dad,
who had such great plans for their
"little angel."

Acknowledgments

Healing Waters: My Trail of Tears from Pain to Peace

They say it takes a village to raise a child. I've found it also takes a village to birth a book. To raise a healthy, well-adjusted child to adulthood, many people need to be involved. It took many people to bring this book from a thought to the words I'm honored to have you read on these pages or hear on this audio. Just as it is nearly impossible to remember everyone who said a kind word to your child, led them by example, taught them, or corrected them when they needed it, I'm certain I'll miss someone who has encouraged me in bringing this book to life. That being said, let me start in no particular order to thank those who helped me make my thoughts, memories, and experiences a book.

Of course I want to thank my husband. Shababa lets me be *me*. He lets me figure myself out and walk the walk I need to walk to be the best me I can be. He supports me as I follow my path. He listens when I need to talk. He cheers when I need to be cheered and he checks me when I need to be checked. He is God's gift to me and I am eternally grateful. Every day, I pray I can provide the same listening ear and unconditional support to him that he gives to me. He gave me the space I needed to heal as I wrote the book and he read my first drafts, always with understanding, compassion, and a complete lack of judgement. Thank you, sweetie, for being you!

I have to thank my parents for loving me and being the best parents they knew how to be. Whatever pain I experienced, curveballs we may have been thrown, or missteps they may have taken, I know beyond a shadow of a doubt that they loved me! I am completely clear that I chose them to be my parents, to learn lessons I needed to learn, to be all I've been called to be. I love them. *My mom and my dad are wholly loved!*

They are loved, forgiven, and released to experience their best lives now and forever.

I want to thank my siblings, Deb and Dean, for loving me every day and being patient with me as I continue to heal and grow. They gave me honest feedback during the writing of the book even while acknowledging that this is, in part, our story, from *my* perspective. Together, we learn to love each other and our parents unconditionally, to be patient with each other, and to listen to each other as we practice being all we can be for each other and for our mom.

I can't end my acknowledgments without thanking my dear friends and coaches, who encouraged me to keep writing and to honor my voice. Some of them took the time from their busy lives to read one revision after another without showing boredom. (Eternal gratitude to Shababa, Pamela, Candace, and Marchell!) My friends encouraged me to cross the finish line when I felt bored and wanted to move on to something else. These include my Triple G and cheerleader, Sheila Reynolds; my dear sister-friend and confidant, Pamela Culpepper; my friend and "speaker of life," Jocelyn Rials; my aunt, friend, and cheerleader, Candy Gellineau-Wilson; my friend and "voice of reason" partner, Dr. Candace Stafford; my writing coach, Kara May; my friend, business and spiritual coach, and sounding board, Marchell Coleman; my early book writing instructor, Vanessa Collins; and my encourager and publisher, Marilyn Alexander. Of course, none of this could have happened without the prompting and guidance of that still, small voice within me that I check in with all day, every day.

Thank you, Village Makers for taking time from your busy schedules to provide your consistent love and support. You each made this journey a little easier and I am forever grateful. Boundless love and respect to you all.

Angel Allen Townsend
2020

Foreword

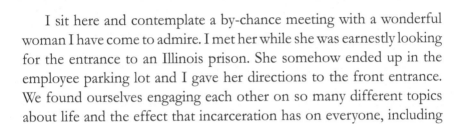

I sit here and contemplate a by-chance meeting with a wonderful woman I have come to admire. I met her while she was earnestly looking for the entrance to an Illinois prison. She somehow ended up in the employee parking lot and I gave her directions to the front entrance. We found ourselves engaging each other on so many different topics about life and the effect that incarceration has on everyone, including family members.

We dove into the subject of how her father came to be incarcerated within the Illinois Department of Corrections system. I touched on the importance of the family structure and how it can be blown apart by incarceration, and she talked about how it changed her entire life. My fascination grew the more we were able to converse. I realized she had an important story to share with the world. The world needs to hear her testimony of courage and how incarceration affects the entire family—not just the incarcerated or the direct victims of crimes. The challenges she faced growing up without her father due to a racially biased justice system led her to learn many lessons through painful trial and error.

My life has taken me from spectator to player in this often unforgiving game of justice. I have seen how families are torn apart when a parent is sentenced to time in the American penal system, thus removing all parts of the traditional family structure, a structure instrumental in preparing children to be productive members of society. Many times we are unaware of the complexities faced by others when they don't directly impact us. We'd do well to show empathy to all parties touched by incarceration.

When men and women are sentenced to prison, they must show toughness in order to survive daily. Prison has a negative impact on their psyche because it strips them of the freedom and ability to show love or compassion. When a person can't practice love, they tend to forget how it feels. These changes occur when people are thrust into an alien environment that promotes violence and prohibits vulnerability.

This experience is a mind-bender that can be hard to recover from. Often, people who have been incarcerated must relearn how to love and be spouses, parents, and friends. The PTSD former prisoners experience when they return to society is comparable to that of a soldier returning home from war. These returning citizens need counseling as they struggle to readjust to civilian life and strive to remain free from the penal system. Men and women must lose the prison mindset and become good parents who demonstrate and teach good values to their children. This can only happen if programs are put in place to support the entire family unit and lessen the negative effects on each family member and the family unit as a whole.

Angel's story and her insights into what went terribly wrong and the processes that might have made her and her family's journey easier are worth serious consideration. My hope is that through her words and the work of many like myself who work on the front lines to effect change, others might be saved from a lifetime of avoidable heartache.

Jacques Buckner
Senior Parole Agent
Illinois Department of Corrections

Endorsements

To read this autobiographical work is to read so many similar stories untold but needing to be told. All too often, these are stories of Black urban female children walking in the darkness that covers dysfunctional families and communities, leading most often to lives destined to be lived desperately. These stories need to be told not because they pull the cover of darkness off of what we know to be the dysfunctional holds within our neighborhoods turned hoods, but rather because they also offer an understanding of the need for lights in the darkness.

Angel Allen-Townsend is a friend, someone I've known for decades, and her story needs to resonate loudly because Angel found enough light to find her way out of the darkness that is inescapable for all too many. In fact, to know Angel today is to know that though stories like hers typically don't end well, as those victimized necessarily succumb to the many and deep scars that have dictated their lives line by line and chapter by chapter, even when there are better angels about.

It is notably a privilege for me to comment on her life story because I myself can remember my Aunt Daisy telling me as an adult, "Bobby, you turned out all right," and I responded that it was thanks to her and others that seeds were planted long ago that couldn't help but flower. Angel's narrative should be a call to arms that we each are responsible to plant, when and where we can, seeds that might just flower and pollinate. Her story is our story, and yes, all stories have the potential to have a happy ending if we write and right ourselves that way.

Robert Bain
Aunt Daisy's Nephew

Most humans spend a lifetime avoiding indictment from a judging public. They put their most acceptable selves on display, as there is often minimal loving redemption when you bare your soul. In this book, not only is it more than cathartic for the author to let go of the burden of truth, but her truth serves as salve to what ails a lot of us as we wrestle with the consequences of our decisions and the grace afforded to us when we surrender.

Pamela Culpepper
she/her
Founding Partner, Have Her Back Consulting

•

Riveting. Raw. Real. Healing Waters is written from a heart of passionate purpose to bring healing and enlightenment to all who have experienced deep levels of trauma. Angel Townsend courageously shares her journey of tragedy, shame and pain and has skillfully produced not only a bestseller, but an educational tool. A must-read for anyone looking to disrupt destructive behaviors that can result from unresolved trauma in both children and adults.

Sheila D. Reynolds, CEO
The Life Changers Group, Inc.

•

This book is a call to action for anyone who needs to understand the hurt that can come from a family member's incarceration and the healing that can be found afterward. A must-read and a captivating read for mental health professionals, clergy, teachers, and those in the legal system and out!

Dr. Candace M. Stafford
Licensed clinical psychologist

•

Contents

Introduction

When I decided to write this book, I knew it would be cathartic. I hoped it might serve to help others glimpse a bit of the destruction incarceration can cause in families if the pain and resulting behaviors aren't interrupted. I hoped some of the thousands of at-risk children in our society might be "saved" or positively impacted, either by reading this book themselves or by a caring adult who might pick it up. Yes, I had high hopes and expectations for this book, but I had no idea how much writing it would affect me in so many ways. I thought I'd worked through most of the biggest hurts I share here, but as I wrote about things I hadn't thought specifically about in decades, it was like pulling the scab off of old wounds. The wounds looked healed from the surface, but once disturbed, the pain felt fresh and the bleeding was profuse. I share specifics here that I'd never told anyone besides the people who were there when the events took place. Discussing these experiences with my husband for the first time was scary at first, but he responded with compassion, understanding and a reassurance that deepened our bond.

My siblings, mom, and I have had many deep, moving, and healing conversations as a result of this work. We have learned things about each other, our feelings, and our experiences during the chaotic years following Daddy's release that we'd never talked about previously. I had conversations with my uncles, cousins, family friends, and childhood friends. Unfortunately, many, many relatives who might have shared fascinating insight into those tough years had passed by the time I embarked on this journey. Some passed during my writing, before I was able to ask them what they remembered about our family during those times, but the conversations I did have were enlightening and healing.

I cried rivers as I remembered, wrote about, and discussed the events shared here. I choose to call these tears "healing waters" because letting go of the pain associated with the memories has allowed room for a freedom I only thought I had before. I've had to ask my family to forgive me because of misplaced hurt and resulting misguided actions, some they shared that I have absolutely no recollection of. I've humbly admitted my missteps to God and the universe and asked forgiveness for any pain or negativity I've released into the world. I've spent a whole bunch of time forgiving myself, nurturing myself, and relearning to love myself, accept myself, and recognize that I *am* forgiven and I *am* loved. In truth, that journey continues.

I decided to write this book with one thought and goal, and that vision remains, but in typical God-fashion: giving from a pure heart and desire to add good to the world, I have been blessed. I have been changed. I *am* being healed.

Preface

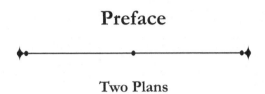

Two Plans

"For I know the plans I have for you, says the Lord. Plans for good and not for evil. To give you a future and a hope." (Jeremiah 29:11)

I've been told that when I was a very young girl of no more than three or four years old, I seemed destined to "do great things." I was smart and curious, outspoken and stubborn. If I wanted it, I went after it, and if I went after it, I usually got it. I came into this world adored by both of my parents; they poured everything they had into me, and later into my younger brother and sister. They taught me how to read and write before I was old enough for school. They played learning games with me and, upon request, read me the same bedtime stories over and over until I could recite them and knew all the words on the pages. They constantly told me I was smart and could do anything I set my mind to. They laid the foundation for me that every child needs: I felt loved and I had a strong, positive sense of self and the courage to go after what I wanted in life. This was the plan for my life, to be healthy and happy, to make a difference in the world in a good way. This was my parents' plan. This was God's plan.

But this was not the way things would go. There was a darker energy at work, a force that wanted me to have none of this. This force also knew the good I could do and wanted to make sure to put up one roadblock after another, to keep me stumbling around in the dark for my entire life. So this enemy of my destiny went to work. This enemy was not, is not, just mine; it aims to destroy any and all, but this was the wave of destruction in my life from my perspective.

Chapter 1

Life Explodes and Darkness Falls

Life changed in an instant

"Mommy, can I have strawberry ice cream *and* orange sherbet at my party tomorrow?" I asked as we turned the corner onto our block. My grandfather was driving us back home from the grocery store where we'd just purchased all my birthday party goodies. I'd just turned six two days before and I was excited about having all my friends and cousins over on Saturday to celebrate.

"Well, I don't know... we got the ice cream already. If your dad or I have time in the morning, we might get back to the store. You've gotta be a good girl, though, and help us out with your brother and sister tonight, okay?"

"Yep! I can't wait for tomorrow! I'm gonna have *so* much fun!"

My grandfather laughed, "You're really excited, huh?" He stopped in mid sentence as we approached our house. My daddy was in our front yard arguing with his friend, Troy.

Daddy had Troy's car door open and as he reached inside, Troy said, "You took my money and you're gonna give it back! I'm not asking, Bill! I don't want to have to kill you!" Troy was yelling and threatening my daddy!

The three of us got out of the car and confused about what was happening, just stood there, watching them.

"Man, I told you I don't have your money! I'm not gonna let you take anything from me! I already told you I didn't take it! What the fuck is wrong with you?!"

Daddy looked up and saw us standing there, trying to figure out what was going on. "Y'all git in the house! I'll be there in a minute!"

My mom and I hurried up the few steps leading to our front door while my grandfather turned and *went back to his car,* saying he was going home to call the police. My grandfather left us! I didn't understand why he didn't take us with him or stay there with us to make sure we were ok. I was really scared. I'd never seen my daddy so mad! Why was Troy shouting at him? What was going on?

They continued to argue as we made our way inside. As my mom and I watched from the front door, they began to fight! Physically fight! My daddy doesn't fight! What was happening?! Troy was trying to take whatever it was that daddy had taken from the car. The fight continued as they found their way onto our front steps.

My mommy and I stood frozen, unable to take our eyes off my daddy and his friend.

"Man, fuck you! I'ma fuck you up!" Troy shouted.

Troy's words were obliterated by the explosion of the thing they were fighting over. Troy dropped right there in front of us, and the three of us, Daddy included, let out a scream of shock. Mommy pulled me to her, burying my face in her dress. I could feel mommy shaking as she cried uncontrollably while she held me.

Time, for me, stopped right then. I was aware of commotion going on around me, but I must have been in shock. Darkness started to fall as my grandfather returned with my grandmother and siblings. My parents, sister, brother and I all huddled in the bathroom together. Daddy sat on the toilet seat and my mother stood, holding his head to her breast as we three children all leaned in close and the five of us just...sobbed.

The paramedics, police, and media all seemed to arrive at the same time. My grandparents knocked on the bathroom door and told us we had to come out.

"Wait, Daddy! Please don't leave me! Please, Daddy, don't go!" I was crying uncontrollably now.

My daddy picked me up and held me tight. "It's gonna be all right, baby," he said. "I'll be back. I love you so much." He pulled my sister and brother into his arms. "You guys be good for your mommy. I'll be back soon. I love you."

He put me down and turned to embrace my mom again. The two of them stood for what seemed like forever, holding each other and crying. Daddy kissed Mommy's tears, kissed her lips, her forehead, her whole face and told her to be strong. Then we watched in horror as they handcuffed my hero, my knight in shining armor, and led him out of the house. We all followed them out, with my grandmother taking the lead, putting her hands out in front of her as she shooed the cameras and microphones out of her face, telling them to leave her family alone.

In a flash, I went from being the happiest little girl in the world to a sad, lonely, scared shell of myself.

Chapter 2

A Miscarriage of Justice

◆———————◆———————◆

*A*t the trial, my father and his younger brother, my Uncle E, testified to the events that led up to Troy's suicide at my father's hands. Earlier that day, at the auto plant that both my daddy and Troy worked at, Troy had been belligerent, loud, and threatening to his coworkers. He had been suspended and told to leave the grounds. Instead, he had waited until the end of the shift and as my father and his friends made their way to the car they would all ride together in, Troy had approached my dad and asked him to ride with him so they could go have a drink.

Choices: Some good

Daddy declined. "Naw, man, I'm just gonna ride with Johnny and them. I'll catch up with you later." The four of them got into Johnny's car and Troy, still mad from earlier in the day, got more annoyed and more insistent.

"Come on, Bill, I just wanna have a drink! I need to ask you something! I need you to do me a favor!" Troy insisted.

"Man, seems like you've had enough to drink already. Why don't you just go home and I'll catch up with you later?" my daddy responded.

Troy got into his car and began to follow Daddy and his friends out of the parking lot and onto the road that would lead them the twenty miles back to Rockford, where they all lived. Troy was honking his horn and yelling for them to pull over so he could talk to my daddy. He was waving a gun and driving erratically. For several miles they tried to ignore him, but Troy kept it up. Daddy, embarrassed by Troy's behavior and not wanting to put his friends in harm's way, finally asked Johnny to pull over.

"Are you sure, man? That white boy is crazy! I don't think you wanna get in the car with him."

"It'll be okay. I think he's just upset about what happened at work today. He probably just wants to talk. I'll see you guys on Monday. Johnny, you're still bringing your daughter to my baby's birthday party tomorrow, right?"

"Yeah, man, we'll be there. Two o'clock, right?"

"Yeah, two o'clock. Don't forget she likes books more than Barbies!" They all laughed as Johnny pulled the car to the side of the road so my daddy could step out.

Choices: Some bad

Daddy got in the car with Troy and they stopped at a liquor store on the way to our house. When they arrived, my Uncle E crossed the street from his house to ours to visit with his brother, as he often did. Uncle E said that Troy put his gun on the table as Troy and Daddy had a beer. Daddy asked to see it and Troy removed all the bullets from it before he handed it to my daddy, who'd never held a gun before that day. Daddy looked it over and handed it back, and they continued talking. When Daddy got up to get more beers from the kitchen, Troy picked the gun up and reloaded it. My uncle testified that Troy always pretended to be Daddy's friend, but Uncle E and their other brothers never trusted him. They said Troy was a troublemaker and Uncle E believed Troy had come to Daddy's house that day to rob him and kill him.

"Troy waved the gun between me and Speed, saying he was gonna kill somebody today because he believed my brother had taken money from him," Uncle E said in court. While the world called my daddy Bill, close friends and family called him Speed because he walked so slow and cool. "Speed told him to calm down and put the gun away before he hurt somebody with it. They kept drinking and I decided to go back home," he testified. Shortly thereafter, he said, he heard what he thought was a gunshot and ran back outside.

Uncle E said Daddy was walking toward him. "I just shot Troy," Daddy told him. "Call the police."

My daddy, well dressed and better spoken, took the stand and told his truth. He, too, testified that he'd only gotten into Troy's car because he was embarrassed by Troy's behavior and didn't want to subject his friends to Troy's nonsense. That Troy threatened him and his family. That he was frightened because Troy was pointing the gun at him and his brother, claiming Daddy had stolen fifty dollars from him, and promised Daddy that "somebody's gonna die before I leave here." That he wasn't familiar with firearms and didn't even remember the gun going off. That he was only defending his family and never meant to hurt Troy. That he just wanted Troy to stop his behavior and go home.

One by one, Daddy's coworkers corroborated Daddy's account of the events, saying that Troy was menacing and they really didn't want Daddy to get in the car with him, but he insisted to keep them out of harm's way.

Every day, my mom sat in that courtroom, usually by herself and as closely behind her husband as she could. She listened intently to every witness and prayed fervently for the miracle that would set my daddy free and allow him to come back home to his family.

Toward the middle of the trial, my amazingly resilient mom picked us up at our grandparents' house after another grueling day of sitting through testimony. When we arrived at home, we found that our house had been broken into. It was an easy target because Daddy's trial was the "story of the day." The newspapers reported on it almost daily, giving a blow-by-blow account of the trial as it unfolded. The stories included pictures of my dad and descriptions of my mom, her demeanor, and her behavior. Because of this, everybody knew our mom would be gone all day. They trashed our home and took our money and belongings. What hurt the most, though, was that they took many of our family photos, which were in a large envelope with other items of value.

Instead of crumbling under the weight of all that was going on, Mom pulled us closer, prayed more, and worked harder. To say she was and is a role model of faith, perseverance, love, and excellence is a massive understatement. To this day, I stand in awe of her strength, commitment, and focus.

Mommy and Grandfather also took the stand. My mom depleted the family savings and borrowed to hire a white attorney to represent my dad. This attorney cashed the checks but failed to advise my mom that she was under no legal obligation to give testimony that could be used to convict her husband. She took the stand and answered the questions truthfully. Clearly, not only was she ill-advised, but she and my father were poorly represented. The prosecution was allowed to ask questions that made Daddy look guilty of murder without so much as an objection from their defense attorney. This black couple in their twenties was no match for a legal system designed to convict—not represent, defend or protect—any black man, and certainly not one who had ended the life of a white man. The fact that it was an accident and an act of self-defense was not considered.

I know taking the stand drained my mom. I imagine it was a painful thing to do. To answer questions that might show her beloved husband in a less-than-ideal light had to be heartbreaking, but what could she do? To say other than what she had witnessed would have been perjury, and my mother is the most honorable woman I know, so that wasn't an option. To her understanding, refusing to testify also wasn't an option, so she did what any black woman in late-sixties America would have done: she answered the questions asked of her and didn't ask questions that she didn't know to ask, questions that might have kept her off that stand completely.

Sadly, years later, my dad told me that during the years he was incarcerated, he nursed hurt and anger against my mother for her testimony, hurt and anger he never revealed to my mother or anyone else. If he had only talked about his feelings with someone, a therapist perhaps, those feelings could have been worked through and he and my mother could have come out on the other side of this tragedy stronger. Instead, that anger festered and became rage and bitterness that we would all suffer from for decades.

No one took the stand for Troy. There were no family members or friends in the courtroom to give even one victim impact statement. Where were his wife, parents, or siblings? Where were his friends or coworkers? There wasn't one tear shed for Troy, which should have served as a strong indication of his character and bolstered the testimonies of the defense, but that was not the case.

After days of testimony and less than three hours' deliberation, my daddy's fate, and ours right along with his, was sealed. My beloved daddy, at only twenty-eight years old, with a loving wife and three children aged six, four, and two, was sentenced to fifteen to forty years in a maximum security prison.

Did this all-white jury not hear anything that was said? Did they not hear about Troy threatening my daddy, his brother, his family, and his friends? Did they not hear that Daddy wanted nothing to do with Troy and tried repeatedly to get away from him? Did they not hear, or did they not care? Did they only see that Daddy, the man left alive, was black and that Troy, although clearly the antagonist, was dead and white?

This is where my mom, at not even thirty years old and with three babies, found herself. Fortunately, my mom is and always has been a fighter. Giving up has never been an option for her. Instead, she enrolled me in first grade and kept working full time. She found a new attorney to appeal my daddy's case and enlisted her parents and my Uncle E to help care for her little ones.

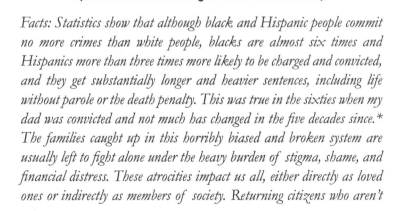

Facts: Statistics show that although black and Hispanic people commit no more crimes than white people, blacks are almost six times and Hispanics more than three times more likely to be charged and convicted, and they get substantially longer and heavier sentences, including life without parole or the death penalty. This was true in the sixties when my dad was convicted and not much has changed in the five decades since.* The families caught up in this horribly biased and broken system are usually left to fight alone under the heavy burden of stigma, shame, and financial distress. These atrocities impact us all, either directly as loved ones or indirectly as members of society. Returning citizens who aren't

prepared to be productive members of society often have a high chance of recidivism, including for crimes that aren't victimless. These men and women and their families often have a greater need for social services, which tax dollars pay for. The vacuum created by an incarcerated parent is too often filled by all the wrong people, activities, and distractions. This can fuel a horrific cycle of poverty, crime, and incarceration that can continue for generations.

Call to Action: We might each consider what we can do to make a difference. Brainstorm with your family and friends about how you can get involved. Please check out *Healing Waters: The Workbook* for suggestions, including organizations and resources that can help you make a difference.

*See endnote

Chapter 3

Mommy

Might we be entertaining an angel, unaware?

I sit in awe of the woman the world calls Yvonne, the woman I'm blessed to call Ma, Mom, or most often these days, Mommy. I think even God might call her an angel.

Mommy came onto this earth in September of 1938, the third child and first daughter of Ivory and Elizabeth, in rural Mississippi during a time when Jim Crow laws were deeply entrenched and strictly enforced, nationwide and especially in the south. Her mom was born in 1910 and her dad in 1915, also both in Mississippi. They migrated north, first to Chicago, then settled in Rockford, Illinois. They were following other family and looking for work.

Once, when my mom was about eleven and returning home from a month-long stay in California, she got off the bus, excited to see my grandmother. Even though they'd never been close and my grandmother was more cold and aloof than warm and affectionate, my mom had missed her. With youthful innocence, she ran to her mom with outstretched arms to embrace her. Remember, this was in the 1940s, so access to phones was minimal. I doubt any letters were passed between them during the four or five weeks she was visiting relatives two thousand miles away.

My grandmother, instead of returning her young daughter's affections, straight-armed her, pushing her away and stunning her into painful silence. If she noticed the hurt and shock on my mom's face, she didn't acknowledge it. She just told my mom to put her luggage in the trunk and get in the car so they could head back home. My mom, over the years, told me this story more than once, never with malice toward her mother, but as a story that impacted her greatly as a child.

11

I believe retelling it might have been an attempt to figure her mom out and work through her own pain.

This story, combined with many others and my own complicated relationship with my grandmother, made me dislike her even more. As I grew older, though, I came to consider what may have driven my grandmother's behavior. I began to reflect on the fact that my grandparents weren't far removed from slavery and indentured servitude. I understand that our ancestors responded to the horrors of slavery in the best ways they could fathom. Some of these responses heaped pain on top of the pain of the atrocities they were attempting to blunt. This sometimes included deliberate detachment or the appearance thereof, from children and other beloved family members, to help get through forced and often sudden permanent separation from each other. Was this behavior adopted to help the children be strong? To avoid giving slaveowners and overseers the satisfaction of knowing the depth of the heart-wrenching pain they caused? To keep from showing weakness in the presence of these cruel masters or their fellow captives?

Whatever the reason, this learned behavior could have easily been passed down through generations. If not showing too much attachment and affection "softened" the blow of separation, but was never explained, processed, or recovered from, it might stand to reason that the children would come to behave in the same manner with their families. Might this have had something to do with my grandmother showing so little affection toward her husband and children—my mother in particular, and later some of her foster children and grandchildren? Or was it something more sinister but basic?

My grandmother didn't seem to like my grandfather much. I never once heard her say a kind word to him. She must have been kind and affectionate toward him at some point; after all, he married her and they had four children. The family joke was those were the four times they had sex! Anyway, my mom looks a bit like her dad and he was always loving toward her. He didn't protect her—and he could have—but he was kind. Did my grandmother hold this against their daughter?

She never explained her mistreatment and anyone who could have given insight into her behavior has taken their knowledge to the grave.

**"You won't believe the way she's always
paying for a debt she never owed."**

Wildflower by Skylark

When my mom was about three years old, her oldest brother James started molesting her. Tragically, this continued until my mom was eleven. When she was in her eleventh year, she started her period, just like I did. This must have scared her twisted brother because he finally left her alone.

Years later, my mom told me he gave her what sounded to me like a half-hearted lie of an apology. He said he didn't "know" what he was doing, that it didn't register with him that what he was doing was wrong. Really? If he wasn't aware that what he was doing was wrong, why did he stop abruptly when his little sister entered her childbearing years?

As if this weren't horrible enough, it is believed that my grandmother had an inkling that something inappropriate was taking place and not only did she not make it stop, but she turned a blind eye to it and treated her molester-son like he created the sun, moon, and stars. She also continued to mistreat my beautiful mom, saying mean things to her, whipping her for the smallest infractions, or simply ignoring her. As if this all weren't sick enough, my grandmother let her son's monstrous behavior continue years later, when he began to molest her foster daughters. She even sent them up to him on more than one occasion.

Somehow, though, my mom kept her quiet, peaceful, and loving spirit and never took her pain out on her younger sister or anyone else. Instead, she protected her baby sister from their brother, taking his abuse so he would never turn his nasty eye toward her.

It takes strength to forgive

Our mom is the epitome of love and forgiveness. It took her years to tell us about what her brother did to her and the fact that her parents didn't stop it. Long before we knew we had a reason to be angry with all of them, my mom took us to see her brother, just like she did many of our relatives. She was careful never to leave us alone with him, but after our daddy was incarcerated, she took us with her to see him at the hamburger restaurant he managed. He was always nice to us and we enjoyed hamburgers and french fries while they talked. Often, he'd pack up bags of food for us to take home. Was this one of the ways Mommy kept us afloat as a single mother with growing children? If it was, we were never the wiser. She acted like it was a treat, a treat we shouldn't expect regularly—we ate mostly simple, but hearty, homecooked meals—and one to politely thank our uncle for giving to us.

My mom was a brilliant student who loved school and she was always at the top of all her classes. She really wanted to be a teacher, but her mother discouraged her constantly and mocked her dreams. When her sister, who was almost four years younger, graduated from high school, she was evidently influenced by my mom's lifelong dream, and she went to college and became a teacher. My mom, who doesn't have a jealous or envious bone in her body, encouraged her along the way. She celebrated her sister's every success in the field she'd loved but been unable to pursue.

Instead of mourning the loss of what she didn't have, she fully embraced another career path. She went to nursing school and became the first black registered nurse to be hired at Rockford Memorial Hospital. She also consistently landed at the top of her classes in her nursing studies and was adored by most of her classmates. She excelled in her field. She eventually opened the first outpatient surgery unit in Rockford at Rockford Memorial Hospital. She was responsible for helping to develop the concept and singlehandedly wrote the operations manual. She also hired and managed the inaugural staff and held this position for years until she retired from her first career in 1996. Along the way, she quietly mentored countless new nurses, most of whom were white, teaching them not only the ins and outs of patient care, but of life and people skills. Many of these women still sing her praises. When my sister especially, as she is also in healthcare, or my brother or I see them around town and they find out we are Yvonne's children, they excitedly share fond memories of our mom.

Call to Action: Many of us may unknowingly carry the pain of our pasts in our bodies, hearts, and spirits. This pain may be generational and so deeply ingrained, it feels like it's in our DNA.* This can be scary or disheartening, but it can be faced and worked through. You can make the difference in your family and community.

Please see *Healing Waters: The Workbook* for books, tips, exercises, workshops and other resources on how to begin this important work.

*See endnote

Chapter 4

The Beginning

◆━━━━━━━━━━●━━━━━━━━◆

Can this love last?

*W*hen Ma first graduated from nursing school, she moved back in with her parents to save money. The Webers lived next door and their children were close in age to our mom and her siblings. The Webers' son, Paul, had a friend who came over all the time to visit. This friend eventually became my daddy. Whenever Daddy visited Paul, he spent more time peeking at my mom than talking to Paul!

Ma was busy with her new nursing career, so at first she didn't pay him much attention. Plus, Daddy really didn't seem like her type. Daddy and Paul drank a little and hung out a lot. It all seemed innocent enough, but Ma didn't drink at all and she hung out very little. Soon enough, though, Daddy's looks, charm, and friendly attitude wore Mommy down and they started dating. Before long, it was pretty serious and they enjoyed each other's company quite a bit, but my mom was unwilling to "go all the way" with my dad, saying she wanted to save herself for her husband.

After almost a year, it seems my dad got frustrated or impatient enough to break things off with my mom. He moved back to Elgin, where some of his cousins lived, and took a job there. I know this sounds unbelievable, but a couple of months later, my mom realized she was pregnant. Yep, that's what I said: no to actual intercourse, yes to pregnancy! Talk about a master plan! My parents always joked that I was destined to be here and somehow make a difference in the world because they never even got to have the all the fun it normally takes to make a baby! It took me forever to understand that joke!

When Mommy called Daddy, they agreed that they really did love each other and they wanted to love and raise their baby together.

Never once have I heard that Daddy questioned Mom's faithfulness or whether I was really his. They both loved me fully from day one. They married on April 6 and moved to Milwaukee, where Mom took a nursing job and Daddy went to work in a dry cleaner's. I was born in Milwaukee, five months to the day later, on September 6. They never told me, maybe because I never thought to ask, but I wonder if they left Rockford to keep nosy, judgmental people from counting the months between their marriage and my birth.

Family members can strengthen a marriage, or . . .

Even though my mom had complicated relationships with her parents and they may not have been affectionate verbally or physically, they loved their family the best way they knew how and my mother loved them back. When my mom and dad moved back to Rockford from Milwaukee, they provided tremendous support to us.

My grandfather owned several houses around Rockford and when we moved back from Milwaukee just over a year after I was born, the three of us moved into one of his smaller homes. This house was one of two that he owned on the same lot. We lived there for a while and as our family grew, we moved to the house on the front of the lot. It was in that house that Troy showed up one day and turned our lives inside out. As the saying goes, we got our "heads busted to the white meat."

After my siblings came along, my grandparents also helped out by babysitting the three of us while my parents worked. When our mom worked nights, as she often did as a nurse, Daddy picked us up at our grandparents' house when he got off work. I remember distinctly one cold winter night when I was about three. He came to pick me up and just stood in the doorway, waiting for me to get my coat on. Why didn't he come all the way inside? He looked uncomfortable. My grandfather stood in the dining room with my dad, making small talk. My grandmother sat in a chair in the bedroom she shared with my grandfather, with me standing in front of her as she buttoned my coat. I could see my daddy from where we were and I was watching his every move. I attempted to pull away from her, saying I wanted my daddy to button my coat. She snatched me right back—hard!

"Be quiet and be still!" she snapped. My daddy just stood there and let her treat me like that! He didn't stop her, but he also didn't scold me for pulling away from her. He just stood there, as did my grandfather. Who was this meanie that two grown men wouldn't stand up to? It was odd, but I was too young to process it. I threw eye daggers at her and forced myself to stand still. Even at that young age, I wasn't afraid of her. The moment she finished buttoning my coat, I dramatically rolled my eyes at her, turned, and ran toward my daddy, yanking my buttons loose as I went. By the time I reached where he stood, he'd stooped down to embrace me, beaming like the sky had just opened up and dripped sun-yellow gold all around us. He laughed, eyes twinkling, as he kissed me on my cheeks and re-buttoned my coat for me. In that moment, both my grandparents melted away, leaving me and my daddy in our own bubble of love. My daddy protected me and I now know that I protected him, too.

Our home was full of love, laughter, and music in the years before the bomb that tore our lives to shreds dropped. Most evenings, once we were all home from work and babysitters, Mommy would head to the kitchen while Daddy turned on music and held me in his arms to dance with me. My siblings, being much younger, were often either in a crib or a high chair. It seemed my regular spot was in my daddy's arms or on his back. I just couldn't get enough of being close to him! As he held me, he'd take Ma's hand and pull her from the pots and pans to join us as we twirled around the room. Both Ma and Daddy would stoop to pick up my sister or brother or plant wet kisses on their cheeks. Sometimes all of Daddy's brothers would pile into our house to hang out, laughing, drinking, and eating Ma's delicious food. My Uncle Fred still talks about how his favorite sister-in-love spoiled him by cooking his favorite meals anytime he asked.

Keep your self-love tank full

Our parents' marriage was mostly good, but there were some early challenges that may have foretold their inability to successfully navigate the storms that lay ahead. Once when I was about two years old, my father told my mother that he was going out to get cigarettes. When he hadn't returned several hours later, my mom got really worried. She called everyone she could think of, looking for him to no avail. I remember (or did she tell me about it years later?) her pacing the floor all night, with me in her arms and Deb in her belly, crying and praying for his safe return. When he still hadn't returned the next day or the day after, she had to return to work, so she took me to her parents' home and did just that. Several weeks later, he returned, acting as if all were normal and he was just back from the corner store with his pack of cigarettes. He'd spent the last few weeks in Florida! He said he needed to get away for a minute to clear his head! Who does that? Who leaves a pregnant spouse with a toddler, telling them he'll be right back, then crosses several states to bask in the sun without so much as a phone call? What does that say about his character? Was Mommy angry? Did they talk about it? Did he apologize and agree to never do anything so disrespectful, inconsiderate, and selfish again?

Whatever he said, Ma accepted it and they fell right back into their daily routines. From my perspective as an adult, I realize now that my mother may have laid the groundwork early on for what my father believed he could get away with. These "agreements" were more than likely unconscious and unspoken, but very real nonetheless.

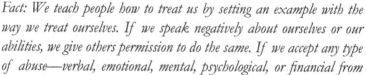

Fact: We teach people how to treat us by setting an example with the way we treat ourselves. If we speak negatively about ourselves or our abilities, we give others permission to do the same. If we accept any type of abuse—verbal, emotional, mental, psychological, or financial from friends, family members, or lovers—even once, we give tacit approval that this behavior is okay and it is bound to continue.

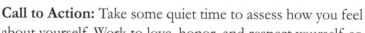

Call to Action: Take some quiet time to assess how you feel about yourself. Work to love, honor, and respect yourself so others will do the same.

Please see *Healing Waters: The Workbook* for specific exercises to bolster your self-esteem and build strong, healthy relationships.

Chapter 5

Daddy

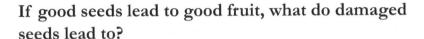

If good seeds lead to good fruit, what do damaged seeds lead to?

I said that our home life was mostly good. Neither of our parents had ideal childhoods and Daddy seemed to struggle a bit more in the aftermath of his than Mom did.

He was the firstborn of his then-unwed mother in rural Tennessee in September of 1939. His mom was tough just like my maternal grandmother and, probably for many of the same reasons, wasn't at all warm and fuzzy. She was proud of the fact that her parents were Native American - her dad was Cherokee and her mom was Chickasaw —and to me, seemed to hold significant color and hair bias.

I'm not totally certain that the only man I knew to be Daddy's father was his biological dad. Daddy seemed to harbor some significant resentment toward his Mom and he carried her maiden name until shortly after he married my mother, when they both changed their last names to my grandmother's married last name, Allen.

Daddy was given his first drink of alcohol by the man he called Daddy and his uncles when he was just nine years old. This set my dad on a lifelong collision course with alcoholism that he mostly kept in check until after he was released from prison.

When Daddy was just sixteen years old, he left Tennessee and moved north to where his cousins lived, near Rockford, to find work. He left his five siblings, four boys and a girl, behind physically but not financially. When he found work in Rockford, he started sending money and clothing back home to help his mom take care of her younger children. Daddy was a hard worker because he had to be. He was also an impeccable dresser and if another life had been available to him, he certainly would have been behind a desk and in charge. Instead, with little formal education, he found himself behind a presser in a dry cleaner's or behind a machine in a factory. Still, it was honorable work and he was an honorable man.

Family members can weaken a marriage

My grandmother loved to tell the story over and over to whomever would listen, that Daddy had another daughter by a young woman, Laura, whose mother thought she was too good for him. This woman forbade them to marry and refused to let Daddy's family stay in touch with the little girl. My grandmother told me this story in a way that made me feel like she wished Daddy had married Laura instead of my mom. Early in my parents' marriage, actually, during their entire marriage, neither my grandmother nor my father's sister were particularly loving toward my mother. Not that my mom ever did anything to deserve this. She was with them the way she is with everyone else: loving, kind, unassuming, and welcoming. Perhaps they had made up their minds not to accept anyone for Daddy if it couldn't be Laura.

My father told me that his sister and the wife of one of his brothers told him while he was still in prison that Mommy had been unfaithful to him. He claims he didn't believe them, but how could that not have weighed heavily on his mind? He was behind bars and his wife was young, pretty, and free. Add the fact that he had long-held misgivings about his parentage and his own mother's fidelity, and we now have a witch's brew wreaking havoc on an already extremely stressful situation. Why would they do that? Why would they add to the already heavy load my parents were carrying? Why would they deliberately cause my dad more sleepless nights, imagining things he could do nothing about? Things that he was probably too scared to even mention to my mother so they could slay that ugly dragon together? Did his sister and sister-in-law laugh about the pain they were causing? Did they hate my mother so much that they didn't care who else might be hurt as long as they sowed seeds of doubt and distrust to hurt her? Sadly, this added fuel to the fire of my daddy's already smoldering anger toward my mom, and all of it was totally unbeknownst to her. To my adult mind, this was particularly calculating and hurtful. Mom kept paying the attorneys to gain Daddy's freedom. She kept money on his books and brought their children to see him regularly. She was devoutly faithful. Daddy, it appeared, only acted the part of a loving, devoted, and appreciative husband.

Several years ago, I had a conversation with Daddy's sister and she told me how she had left Tennessee to join us in Milwaukee.

"I moved in with you guys to help my brother out. I came to take care of you while they both worked," she said.

"You mean, you came to help both of my parents out, right?" I asked her.

"No, I came to help my brother."

"Wow!" I thought. "How small and petty is that?!" But with all the grace and diplomacy I'd learned from my mom, I said, "So you were my first babysitter! We should be so much closer than we are! We should work on that!"

"Yeah, we should," she responded dryly.

I've never had any hard feelings toward her, my grandmother or any of my father's peeps, and they were always kind enough to me and my siblings. The beauty is that both my grandmother and my aunt eventually fully embraced my mom. My mom never wavered in her unconditional love, acceptance and forgiveness. We visited them on many occasions and they and their families were present at many of our family gatherings, including several birthday parties we gave in my mom's honor. They always came bearing gifts and full of love. Once again, it's proven that love always wins.

Having said that, my father's brothers were always great. They all loved my mom and they loved us. We loved them all right back. Too bad I can't say the same for his dad, my grandfather. If he were still alive and walked into this room right now, if not for family resemblance, I'd have no idea who he was. He never tried to have a relationship with me; he never tried to fill the gap left by my father's incarceration. I don't remember having even one conversation with him, ever. The saying that you can't miss what you never had is not always true. The imagination is powerful and I miss what I imagine could have been a helpful, healing, nurturing relationship with a grandfather.

A few times during Daddy's incarceration, we were allowed to go to Tennessee to visit my grandmother and my dad's two youngest brothers. I loved all of my uncles, but my Uncle Lannie seemed to be as drawn to me as I was to him. He hugged me, talked to me, and made me feel like he "saw" me. He reminded me of my dad and I was by his side as much as I could be every time I saw him. For me, spending time with my Uncle Lannie was the highlight of our visits to Tennessee.

Another midnight sky in the middle of the day

One late summer afternoon, when I was about eleven years old, our phone rang.

"Hey Uncle E," I said when I heard his voice.

"Hey Ang, let me speak to your mom." His voice didn't have its usual easy lilt.

"Sure, let me get her." I wanted to ask why he sounded the way he did, but I knew better and called for my mom to pick up the phone.

I watched her closely to see if I could figure out what was going on. She was quiet, shaking her head slowly, as if in disbelief.

"Okay, yeah, I'll tell them. I'll get in touch with Bill, too. How's your mom? Do you need anything?"

I was a little nervous because of what I was hearing from her end of the conversation. What could have happened?

"Okay, let me know about arrangements. I'll talk to you tomorrow."

When she hung up the phone, she told me to come sit beside her. I did. "What's wrong, Mommy? What happened?"

"Sweetie, your Uncle Lannie had a blood clot earlier today and he passed just a little while ago."

"No way! That can't be right! Are you sure? I didn't get to talk to him! He was gonna call me soon! He told me he would call me!" I was near hysterics. This didn't make sense to me! He was only in his early twenties. How could he be dead?

My mom held me as I sobbed into her shoulder. "What happened?" I asked when I was finally able to speak again.

"His leg was bothering him. He collapsed and they took him to the hospital, but by the time they got someone to see him, it was too late. I'm so sorry, honey. I know how much he meant to you."

My mom, ever the strong woman I've always known her to be, put her feelings aside to comfort me. I'm sure she wondered, at the same time, how she was going to break the news to my daddy about his younger brother's transition. How would he take this blow, knowing that he wouldn't be allowed to attend the funeral or be there to comfort his family? Daddy's unjust incarceration had such far-reaching effects on every part of our lives. I just wanted him home. We all did.

Courage under fire

While my father was incarcerated, he may have been harboring resentment, but he was an exemplary inmate. He got his associate's degree in Business Management. He taught classes in English and other subjects to fellow inmates. He started a JayCee's Chapter and was its president for several years. In most ways, he did what all inmates are encouraged to do: he used the time instead of letting the time use him. I could try to figure out the glaring contradictions in my father's behavior. I could try to make sense of some of his responses to my many probing questions. I could ask his friends or surviving family members to help me understand. In the end, though, I think acknowledging and accepting that we're all complex and flawed human beings sums it up best.

I'm very aware that although this chapter is called "Daddy," I don't say much about who I really knew him to be. Sadly, this is because most of my knowledge of him is from before he was taken from our day-to-day lives. The "good" daddy I knew later in life was, at best, fragmented because I was an adult living in another city and missed the opportunity to know him fully by living under the same roof with him.

Call to Action: All marriages can benefit from the loving support of family members. This is especially true if the marriage is facing challenges such as incarceration, homelessness, addiction, domestic abuse, etc. Consider ways you might support your children's, siblings', or even friends' marriages.

Please see *Healing Waters: The Workbook* for exercises, conversation starters, and suggestions on how you can help build strong marriages in your family and community.

Chapter 6

The New Normal

$\blacklozenge$—————$\blacklozenge$—————$\blacklozenge$

"She may be quiet, but she's a warrior and her prayers can move mountains."—Unknown

*S*hortly after Daddy was snatched from our lives, we moved to a two-unit house across the street from my maternal grandparents. God bless them and my Uncle E. At only nineteen years old, he selflessly took the unit upstairs from us. This way he could help my mom with his nieces and nephew. He babysat us while Mom worked or went to see the attorney. He made sure we were safe and fed. When he had to work, my grandparents stepped right in and provided care, discipline, and meals. My father has another brother who also stepped up. As I got a little older, my father's brother, Uncle Fred, and his wife, my Aunt Jessie, invited me into their home any weekend I wanted to stay. They'd cook me good food and buy me *Right On!* magazines to read late into the night in the guest room they made up especially for me. My mom's village drew close to prop us up and love us all through the nightmare that had become our life.

Our new neighborhood was full of kids and soon we were just part of the group. Our grandparents had always fostered children and when we moved across the street, they had two sisters living with them: Charlotte was my age and Shirley was two years older. They had also adopted a girl, Lynn, who was two years older than me as well. Even though Lynn was technically our aunt, because of her age, all of them became like sisters to the three of us, and for years either we were at their house or they were at ours.

During the summers, we played outside from early morning until the streetlights came on. Then we played late into the evening in either ours or our grandparents' yard under the watchful eye of them, our mom, or our Uncle E. If it rained or got too cold to be outside, we played board games or told scary stories in our grandparents' basement.

Visiting Daddy

Within a year, we were making twice monthly visits to see our daddy at Stateville Correctional Facility, a maximum security prison in Joliet, Illinois. As I mentioned, my mom had a decent job as a registered nurse and always had a side hustle selling Avon or Tupperware. We never spent one day on welfare, but she used every extra dime she could come up with on either my father's defense or putting money on his books so he could get things he needed from the commissary. Because of this, our car was old and not in the best shape. Even so, every other Saturday, the four of us piled in to make the hundred-mile drive from Rockford to Stateville. To keep our car from overheating, we had to stop several times during the trip so Mom could add water to the radiator from one of the jugs she kept in the trunk.

My mom made the best of those trips. The four of us sang songs or listened while our mom made up funny stories to tell us. She taught us to sing our parts to "Row, Row, Row Your Boat" or "Are You Sleeping, Brother John?" We'd all crack up laughing as we tried to come in on cue for these "in the round" songs. When we were still making these trips years later, we'd play "That's My Car!" as newer, fancier cars passed us along the way, or the four of us would take turns adding to stories that Ma started. She was always so creative and encouraged us to use our minds to think, imagine, and dream.

When we arrived at the prison parking lot, we gathered up our dolls and books to keep us occupied while we sat in the visitors' room waiting for our name to be called so we could see our daddy. Then we took the walk that we all came to dread through the visitor gates of the hell my daddy had to call home. Mom wrote our names in the visitors book and we took our seats to wait. After what seemed like hours, a voice would boom over a loudspeaker.

"Visit for Allen. Visit for Allen. Sixty two six eighty three. Visit for Allen"—62683 was my daddy's inmate number. That number, after all these years, is still etched into my memory like I just heard it yesterday.

We stood and a guard—I understand they prefer to be called "officers" now—led us through the door into the prison. We were then ushered into a room where all four of us, even my baby brother, who wasn't yet three when we started these visits, were unceremoniously patted down to ensure we weren't bringing contraband in to our daddy. This was so embarrassing and intrusive. I didn't have the words for it at the time, but it felt like I was being molested.

Why did this guy have to pat down my entire body just so I could see my daddy?

Why were all these people watching our every move?

Why did Mommy suddenly look so sad every time we passed through these doors?

Why did most of the people in the waiting room look like us?

Did only black people have to live here? None of this made sense to my little-girl mind and nobody was taking the time to help me understand this strange new world we found ourselves trying to exist in.

Once they had determined we weren't criminals, they led us through more clanging doors and gates to the visitation room. As we went through the final door, my beautiful daddy was coming through an identical door facing us.

"Oh, my God! There he is!" It was all I could do to not make a break for it and run into his arms! Tears streamed down my face as my mommy held my hand to keep me calm. His grin was my sunshine and I was again sure that I was loved. He grinned and waved and blew kisses to all of us.

He turned right into the visitors' room and we turned left into the same room. Just inside the entrance sat another guard at a big desk. These creepy creatures were everywhere—dang! But by now I didn't care. I knew I was gonna be embraced by my daddy. I knew I was gonna feel his arms around me. I knew I was gonna smell his Speed Stick aftershave. I knew I was gonna hear him whisper in my ear how glad he was to see me and how much he loved me and missed me. No, in this moment all I could see was my daddy!

A couple of steps down from the big desk where the guard sat was a low glass wall. This was where the inmates and their families were allowed to greet each other under the intrusive eye of the guard and probably many cameras.

First Mommy and Daddy warmly embraced. They kissed each other softly, touching their foreheads together and whispering things we couldn't hear. Then Mommy picked my brother up for Daddy to hug and kiss him. Then she did the same with my sister. The whole time Daddy was grinning from ear to ear, his eyes glistening with the joy of seeing his family.

When my turn came, in my regular, bold fashion, I stood on the stool by myself and practically jumped into my daddy's arms! God, I could have stayed right there forever and been perfectly content!

Finally, my daddy pulled me away from his neck to gaze into my eyes. "Boy, you get prettier and prettier every time I see you!" he laughed and kissed me on my cheek again before putting me down so we could start our visit.

We went down a few more steps, us on one side, Daddy on the other, and walked along the long row of families and involuntary guests of Stateville until we found open seating across from each other.

Only two visitors were allowed to sit at the window at a time, so my mom sat with one of us kids and the three of us took turns. My sister and brother were younger and hadn't yet formed that "Daddy's my king and can do no wrong" bond with him, but he *was* my king and I wanted to sit there the whole time, gazing into his eyes, trying to soak up as much of him as I could to keep me going for the two weeks before I could see him again. My siblings seemed content to sit and play, Deb with her Barbie doll and Dean with his G.I. Joe, but Mommy and Daddy made me trade places with them so Daddy could enjoy them, love them, and absorb their essence, too, and they could receive all of that in return. Even though I reluctantly gave up my seat, I really did want them to know and love Daddy as much as I did. He was *our* king and they deserved his love, too!

Far too soon, the end of our visit was announced by the guard sitting at the front of the room. We all shed a tear as Daddy told us to be good and "do what your mommy tells you to do."

We moved toward the front of the room in unison and when we arrived at the short window again, we were allowed to say our goodbyes with hugs and kisses. I usually had to be pulled from Daddy's arms by my mommy as she wiped my tears and hers. Daddy stood, helpless to stop my pain, and wiped away tears of his own. We headed up the same steps we'd come down just two short hours before and walked out the door. As we turned to our right to leave the area, Daddy turned to his left to go back to untold horrors. We all stopped and turned to blow each other kisses and mouth "I love you" to each other. We didn't turn away until the doors clanged shut, blocking our view of my beloved daddy and blocking his view of the family he adored.

The ride home was always a lot more solemn. My sister and brother played quietly in the backseat while Mommy and I sat in the front, lost in our own thoughts. I looked out the window, crying softly, while Mommy stared straight ahead, blinking back her own tears. Every now and then, she reached over to squeeze my hand in that special, reassuring way she had that made me believe somehow things were gonna work out.

I think both Mommy and I waited anxiously for the weekly calls and letters we received from Daddy. A few times a week, a letter would arrive for one of us, confirming that Daddy loved and missed us as much as we did him. To this day, I still cherish the beautiful cards covered with pictures of fairytale princesses and filled with words of love, encouragement, and hope that he sent me. And hearing his voice over the phone was always the highlight of my week. None of that, though, could replace his everyday presence that I constantly prayed for. "Please, God, when will You let my daddy come home to us?"

"Many hands make light work." Tanzanian Proverb

When we got back home, we obediently fell into our regular routines. Because of the example of excellence our mom set for us every day, we all pitched in to make the best of things. We were a team and we knew it. As the oldest, I took the responsibility of taking care of my brother and sister seriously. When we had to walk to school in winter, more than once I held Deb's hand while I carried my brother on my back when the snow was too deep for him to navigate.

And, more than once, our grandfather passed us by, heading to the same school we were trudging through the snow to get to, with his car full of his girlfriend's kids. My eyes stung with tears from hurt and anger, but I held my head high and kept walking. This wasn't the first time our grandfather abandoned his children. This seemed to be his pattern. He didn't protect his daughter when she was a child from her brother or her mother or later, his foster daughters from the same abuse. He also chose to leave this same daughter, my mother and his granddaughter, me, alone to fend for ourselves when my father and Troy fought over a gun with live ammunition. While I appreciate all the ways he did show up for us, I can't help but wonder how his lack of protection in the aforementioned ways impacted us all on a subconscious level. Did the way he, my father and most of my uncles *not* show up for me impact my feelings about men in general and my romantic relationships in particular?

As we got older, mom made sure we could put simple meals together. After school, we'd let ourselves in and make "poor man's stew" or grilled cheese sandwiches with tomato soup, then do our homework and chores before we went outside to play. We were never out of shouting distance of either our grandparents or our Uncle E.

It wasn't all work and no play, though. Not only did she take us on fun excursions, but our mom always made sure there was plenty of joy and laughter in our home. Many evenings and cold or rainy afternoons, when mom wasn't working late, the four of us played games. Our Ma used these opportunities for us to bond, laugh, and learn. When we played Pick-Up Sticks, she taught us about being patient and strategizing, both skills needed to decide which sticks to pick up without disturbing the others and hopefully win the game! When we played Pitty Pat, a card game, we learned to count, add, and subtract. Of course, we also played Scrabble, each of us with a dictionary at our side so we could spell words that would get us the biggest scores, and Monopoly, where we also learned to count and rack up the most properties. Mom even played jacks with my sister and me. We had so much fun trying to pick up as many jacks as possible in our little hands, and somehow we usually seemed to win.

All the while, we were taught more subtle lessons like taking turns, being respectful of each other, winning *and* losing graciously, and listening when others talked. Even though we were learning, we shared plenty of uproarious laughter! If one of us decided to pout because we had lost, my mom sent us to our room with a big smile and usually a peck on the cheek, saying, "It's just a game, honey! Relax! We'll be right here having fun; come back and join us as soon as you're ready!" After a few minutes of listening to the laughter and not wanting to miss out, whichever of the three of us had retreated to our room was back and the games continued! The only thing missing from this nearly perfect picture was the daddy and husband we all yearned for.

"I'll be home for Christmas, if only in my dreams"
Kim Gannon

At Christmas, we'd put up our big artificial tree together, pop and string popcorn, and sing Christmas carols as we decorated it. On Christmas morning, we had *so* many presents under the tree! We couldn't wait to start opening them. The three of us always had at least one huge box under the tree and my mom always handed each of us one of those boxes first. Then she'd take her seat and could barely contain her laughter as we tore off the newspaper funnies section she'd creatively used as wrapping paper. When we got the paper off and opened the box, we found that it contained yet another box. Curiously, we took that box out and opened it. This box, too, contained a box. What could it be? By now, Mommy was doubled over with laughter. What was so funny? When we opened the last box, usually in unison, we found either an old Chuck Taylor gym shoe that we'd thrown away months before or a big rock from the yard!

"Mommy!" we'd all say together. Then the three of us would burst out laughing, too, as much at the joke as at how hilarious our mom thought she was. Yeah, she always found a way to add some humor to our lives!

About the time we finished opening gifts, we got the best present of all. Daddy called and we each got a few minutes to tell him about our gifts: an Easy-Bake Oven for me, a Buffy vanity set for my sister, a train set for my brother, and books and clothes for all of us, along with our prank gifts. Then Mommy took the phone into her bedroom so she and Daddy could talk privately for a few minutes. Even though we didn't see our dad on Christmas, both of our parents did a great job of including him in our day and for that I will forever be grateful.

+————————————◎————————————+

Fact: When children are disappointed or neglected enough by primary caregivers they can learn to disassociate themselves from primary relationships, exhibiting characteristics of attachment and other emotional disorders that have sometimes been known to result in violent behaviors.*

+————————————◎————————————+

Call to Action: Regularly "taking temperatures" in relationships keeps them strong. This is particularly true when life-altering events such as incarceration, sudden moves, homelessness, death, etc. take place. Please ask your children and your partner how they're feeling about the changes taking place in your lives. If they aren't ready and willing to talk, think of creative ways to start conversations or get them to share.

*See endnote..

Please see *Healing Waters: The Workbook* for exercises and suggestions on how to start and continue these healing conversations.

Chapter 7

People: Some Good, Some Completely Tone Deaf

No words required; your actions drown them out anyway

*W*hen we moved and Mom needed her parents to help out with us more, we started going to church with them. As a registered nurse, Ma worked odd hours. Weekends were the same as any other day at the hospital and along with second, third, or swing shifts, Mom worked most Sundays.

Rockford is a small town and the tragedy that took place between Daddy and Troy was common knowledge. In the black community, though, almost everyone knew it was *our family* that this happened to. (The population at the time was approximately 147,000. About 15 percent were black.) I think it might be more common now that almost everybody has a family member or knows someone whose loved one is or has been incarcerated, but in the late sixties and early seventies in Rockford, it wasn't common at all. Even so, the only person who ever openly tried to shame us because of our heartache was my grandparents' adopted daughter Lynn. We were never treated differently or in any way singled out in church because of what we were going through.

We sang in and traveled with the youth choir. Every year we took a trip to Memphis, Tennessee for the Church of God In Christ annual convention. We had no idea how honored we were to take choir lessons from Mattie Moss Clark and her daughter Twinkie. We learned so much from them and other lesser-know, but great choir directors. My biggest influence, though, came from my home choir director. To this day I'm grateful to our choir director, a beautiful soul we all affectionately call Aunt Cle. She believed in us, encouraged us, and loved us. She felt like shelter in a storm. I sang in the second soprano section and once, during choir practice, Aunt Cle asked me to sing a line by myself! I was never comfortable singing alone and I hesitated.

Aunt Cle was confident I could do it and she insisted. "Angel, we're not moving on until you sing this line! Come on, baby, I know you can do it," she said gently but firmly. With everyone watching me, I figured it was better to just face my fears and get it over with, so I took a deep breath and sang the line, hitting the notes perfectly! To my surprise, everyone cheered! Aunt Cle looked at me with a big smile on her face and in her eyes. She gave me a wink as she turned back to her son on the organ and told him to start the song from the beginning. I was on top of the moon and my insides felt like they were being warmed by the sun. Thank you, Aunt Cle, for your unwavering love and support.

There were other adults at church who loved us, too. They hugged us, invited us home to hang out with their children, and fed us. That being said, there was still a huge void in my life where my daddy should have been all the time, not just maybe a couple of dozen times, only forty-eight hours at the most, a year.

Two of my father's younger brothers and our maternal grandparents were all there for us, and for that I am grateful. But the conversations I know I missed; the daily adoration of my daddy to help me develop into a healthy, secure young woman; the opportunity to witness a loving, healthy marriage up close; and even the scolding of a caring, involved dad were all absent from my life. I think I might have missed these things more than my brother and sister because I had more consciously spent time with him at home before our lives changed. It's harder to miss what you never had, so Deb and Dean were never as sad as I seemed to be all the time.

No man stepped in to try to fill that void. Nobody ever really gave me a "heart" or "spirit" check by asking me how I was doing, what I was thinking or feeling, or whether I wanted to talk about what was happening with my daddy. Was it because Mommy kept Daddy involved, even from afar, and made it clear that her eyes, body, and heart belonged to him? What about men who had no romantic interest, but genuinely cared about the mental health of their friends' children or members of their family, of their community? Where were they?

Did they not know how to approach our mom about us? Did they have their hands full with their own children and lives? Did they just not care?

Mommy did her part, for sure. She found the time and energy to take us to visit our aunts and uncles and their families. She put us in the presence of men who could get involved, but for the most part they didn't. (Again, my father's brothers, our Uncles E and Fred, and our maternal grandfather were the exceptions.) This isn't an indictment; I long ago released any resentment for some perceived slight and fully appreciate each of them for any kind word or hug they may have shared or for just treating us like every other kid they knew. No, this is observation from the long lens of hindsight, recognition of what might have made our journey just a little easier.

> **Call to Action:** As Vernon Johns, predecessor to Dr. King as pastor of Dexter Avenue Baptist Church, said, "If you see a good fight, get in it." This is what I ask anyone reading this book to do. If you know of any at-risk children, whether they have a parent missing from the household or live in an unstable environment, engage them—with the knowledge and consent of their parents and in a professional, acceptable, and safe way. Mentor them, talk with them, and help them to process and successfully navigate their experiences and feelings. Healthy children make healthy adults, and this benefits us all.

Please see *Healing Waters: The Workbook* for tips and exercises on how to get involved with mentoring children in your area.

Adjust, adapt, try to overcome

An unexpected side effect of the gut-punch that shook our family to its core was that my speech suddenly changed. I began to stutter and speak with a lisp! Was I traumatized? Was I just nervous and stressed? I don't know, but my "st" became a "th," so what should have been "first" came out "firth" and I could barely finish a sentence without stuttering. I became quieter and more withdrawn, brokenhearted because I missed my daddy and embarrassed because of the way I talked. I still did well in school, so except for my mom working with me to improve my speech at home, my impediment went unaddressed. That is, until my astute, caring third grade teacher, Mrs. Williams, intervened.

"Angel, I'm going to talk to your mom about it, but I want you to see the school speech pathologist." Mrs. Williams, one of my favorite teachers, was strong, firm, confident, and regal, the magnificent color of rich dark chocolate, with a rich, melodic voice to match. "I know you've got a lot to say and she can help you say it with confidence!" she continued, her beautiful brown eyes glistened with genuine concern and affection as she spoke with her hand resting gently on my arm. "Would you be okay with that?" she asked.

How did she know how badly I wanted to express myself more clearly but just couldn't seem to get the words out?

I smiled back shyly. "Ye-ye-yeth. Th-th-that would be great!"

"Okay. I'm going to call your mother and we'll get you set up for sessions during recess so you don't have to stay after school," she said as she drew me in and hugged me tight. She smelled like flowers and felt like I imagined my grandmother would if she ever hugged me. "You're so smart, Angel. I know this is going to be really good for you!"

I was a little scared, but more excited. I was ready to have my voice back, but would it work?

Mrs. Williams called my mom and, of course, she agreed to let me see the pathologist. We got to work the following week and within the year I was no longer stuttering and my lisp was almost gone.

I recently asked my sister Deb about Mrs. Williams and we agreed that after we left grade school, we never heard about her again. Perhaps she just moved on to a new school in a new city, but I think she was yet another angel God placed in my life to ease my way, like a cool drink on a hot day.

Our mom truly was, and is, amazing. With all she had on her plate, she stayed involved in our lives. She always helped us with homework and went to PTA meetings. She enrolled us in every activity she could find. When I realized I had a love and an aptitude for gymnastics, she found a gym and enrolled me in private lessons! Then, if she was off that day, she'd wait patiently while I had my lesson, cheering me on when I did a perfect backflip and encouraging me to try again when I fell. Those countless hours in the gym with my instructor, Peggy, served me well when I tried out for and made the Pom Pom and cheerleading squads. I absolutely loved being a part of those squads! Most of the girls were great, the camaraderie was just what I craved, and the physical outlet, excelling at something I thoroughly enjoyed, released healthy endorphins.

When Deb decided she wanted to model, our mom fully supported her in that, taking her to her classes and later traveling with her on modeling assignments.

Dean found karate and she gave him the same love, support, and attention with that. Amazingly, she was also a den mother for Dean's Boy Scout troop, going with him each week to support his growth and pour into the other young boys in the troop, too. Again, it would have been such a blessing had any uncle or other family friend stepped in to mentor our brother, but our mom, in regular Yvonne fashion, didn't whine about what wasn't. She filled the roles to the best of her ability, put on a happy face, and instilled in each of us to not make excuses but make plans and keep it moving.

Deb and I were both Brownies and then Girl Scouts. She and I played piano and Dean played the guitar. We had a piano to practice on between lessons and Mom made sure we practiced before she took us to our lessons each week. Dean had a new guitar and weekly lessons. She listened as he practiced or played the latest piece he'd written.

I think my brother got the bulk of the natural musical talent in our family. He never took piano lessons but he and Mom, by far, play the best of the five of us. He also rocked that guitar! He just has an ear for music. Who knows what he might have done with it if not for the devastating storm that was brewing ahead?

We also spent a lot of time at the local swimming pool and the community center. Every fall we went to an apple orchard to pick apples, go on hayrides, and enjoy warm apple cider and yummy, freshly made apple donuts. Mommy took us, and our three "sisters," Lynn, Charlotte, and Shirley, to amusement parks, museums, and events and presentations for children. Yep, we were, more often than not, the only chocolate babies there, but Mommy didn't care. She wanted us to be exposed to and involved in as much as possible. We had a very active and fulfilling childhood. I think Mom's goal was to not just try to fill the void left by my father's absence, but to ensure we got the healthy, happy childhood she'd always envisioned for us despite the curveball we'd been thrown.

Our mom loved to read and she encouraged this same love in all three of us children. Our home was filled with books, including a set of encyclopedias. Anytime we had a "but, why?" question – "why is the sky blue?" "why do cows have spots?" – she sent us to the encyclopedias to find out. I read everything I could get my hands on. If it had words on it, I read it. I'd wake up before dawn, make a fried bologna sandwich and take my book to the back porch to read as the sun rose. Hours later, when the house started to stir, this is where my mom would find me. Sometimes, late at night, my sister would reach her hand up from her lower bunk to pull the chain that turned off the light so she could sleep. Usually, I'd just take a flashlight and continue reading under the covers so I wouldn't disturb her. Reading was my way of escaping the harsh reality of my daddy's absence.

There was a social group in town designed to help young girls be their best and expose them to ideas and activities they might not otherwise know. I really wanted to be a part of Taus Inc. There was an application process and my mom, as usual, was all in. She helped me complete the application. She helped me select a dress and we rehearsed the short speech I'd have to give as part of my interview. I was ready! When we arrived, I immediately felt the snobbish negative energy from the women who would conduct the interviews and choose the new members. This energy was especially strong from one of the officers, Mrs. Merks, who had also been my sister's grade school teacher. She seemed to look down on me and my mom. My mom demurred and quietly took her seat. This was unlike her and it unnerved me a bit, but I brushed it off, determined to do my best and wow them with my poise and presentation. I did a great job! I was prepared. I spoke clearly and confidently. I answered their questions with assuredness. My mom sat beaming at me. I could tell she was proud of me and I could feel her love surrounding me like sunlight. Mrs. Merks and the other interviewers, on the other hand, barely smiled and gave only half-hearted applause when I finished. I wasn't accepted.

Even though I wasn't surprised, I was crushed. Maybe they could only accept so many girls and I just didn't make the cut, but in my ten-year-old mind, their smug and dismissive behaviors toward me and my mom made me feel that they didn't think we were good enough because my daddy was incarcerated for protecting himself and his family. I know there were other women in the room, but Mrs. Merks was the most openly unpleasant and I aimed all of my displeasure at her. It took me decades to truly forgive her. I now choose to believe she had no idea that she delivered a gut punch that bruised my spirit, if not my body. I've been told she's experienced several tough personal blows in recent years. I imagine she's developed humility. My prayer is that she has learned to extend compassion to those who cross her path.

Our mom has always provided a nearly flawless example of how to treat others—with kindness, respect, and consideration. But my experience with Mrs. Merks and Taus Inc. drove home the point my mom exemplified. While it was clear that she had no concern for me, the pain Mrs. Merks inflicted made me vow, even at that young age, to never treat others like I think I'm better than they are, and I never have.

Hope in the midst of it all

When I was ten or eleven, Daddy was allowed, as part of a group he was involved in at Stateville (probably the JayCee's), to attend the state fair in Springfield. We were so excited! We were gonna get to spend time with Daddy outside the stinky smells and clanging gates of the prison. We were gonna get to hug him and spend time with him *outside* in the sunshine! We were all practically floating as we dressed and packed light lunches for the three-hour trip from Rockford to Springfield.

I was a little nervous, too. How would we feel without being under the never-ending gaze of the cameras and the guards in the visiting room at Stateville? I needn't have worried. When we saw him on the grounds, he scooped us up in his arms one by one, laughing, hugging, and kissing us all at the same time!

He looked at our mommy like she was truly his joy, and that gave me joy! Lord, I begged silently, can we just live on the state fairgrounds forever? Can we stop time? My whole family together! This is heaven! We laughed and talked while we went from booth to booth, almost oblivious to the guards always nearby. Daddy was, after all, still in the custody of the state.

By this time, I'd begun collecting coins and had some really nice, old ones at home. My daddy, always aware of what we were into, found a collector on the grounds and helped me pick out several that he wanted to buy for me to add to my collection. This was what I missed by my daddy being away from us. My heart was bursting with love and excitement! Daddy told the man what coins he wanted to get for "his angel" and then completed the transaction.

Because our visit was sadly coming to an end, Daddy told me he'd have the man wrap them up and he'd ship them to me at home. A few weeks later, the package arrived ripped and empty. I didn't care so much that the coins had gone missing, but that it was something from my daddy and a symbol of our time together and that special memory was stolen from me.

We were both saddened by this event and my daddy apologized over and over during our next phone conversation. I knew even then that it wasn't his fault. I didn't blame him. It became clear that he was helpless to protect me and although I didn't realize what was happening or have words to articulate it, I was becoming angrier and more depressed as each blow landed squarely to the center of my soul.

Fact: Apologies, while important, are not enough. The incarcerated parent and the custodial parent must both speak from a position of power, strength, and confidence.

Call to Action: Maintain awareness of how you speak around and to your children. Speaking positively and confidently, with an eye toward a healthy future, can help ward off feelings of sadness and hopelessness.

Please see *Healing Waters: The Workbook* for suggestions and exercises that can help you and your children maintain positive outlooks and ways to plan and prepare for the time when your entire family will be together again.

Chapter 8

I See You

Don't start none, won't be none!

The street that separated our house from our grandparents' home was a side street that wasn't well traveled. It was the perfect spot for the dozens of kids in our neighborhood—and those who came from across town because our block was poppin'!—to gather to play baseball, run relay races, or race each other on our bikes.

More than once, my adopted "aunt" Lynn, who was more like a sister to us, waited until the street was full of kids so she could demand that everybody be quiet and then bellow out, "Angel's daddy in jail!" She only got half the effect she was looking for. Most of the kids just looked at her like she was scratching, grunting, and jumping around like an ape in the jungle, but she was landing daggers in my spirit.

She may have been a bully, but I was never afraid of her. She regularly beat up her sisters, Charlotte and Shirley, and they never put up much of a fight. If I was around, though, I jumped right in and tried to knock her head off. Pent-up aggression, I guess.

She never challenged me straight up. No, she didn't have that much heart. Once, she called me over to "look at something" and when I got close, she struck a match, blew it out, and touched it to my face, burning me. I yelled out in pain while she laughed uncontrollably. Rather than fight her then, I plotted my revenge. Later that month, when she thought I'd forgotten about it, I took matches and a Styrofoam meat container and called her to come and see some newborn bunny rabbits in our backyard.

"Where?" she asked as she looked under the bushes I'd pointed to.

"Right there," I answered, giving myself time to strike the match and set the Styrofoam on fire.

"I don't see anything," she said as she stood up to face the flaming Styrofoam. Before she could say another word, I'd thrown the entire thing on her, burning her face and singeing her hair. Years later those visible scars remained.

"You thought I forgot, huh? That's what you get! I told you to stop fuckin' with me!" I said to her as she frantically beat the fire out in her hair, screaming and crying in pain.

"What's wrong with you? You crazy bitch!" she yelled.

I ignored her and calmly walked around to the front of the house, went inside, and shut the door. From then on, at least the nasty remarks in front of our friends pretty much stopped. Bullies don't like to be stood up to.

Besides Charlotte, my best friend was Rosena, or Rose for short. She and her brother and sister lived at the end of the same side street we all gathered on to play. The three of us spent countless hours together upstairs in Rosena's and her sister Thomasina's room, listening to music, singing every word to every song, and talking about what we would do when we got old enough to be out on our own.

A turning point

I was thirteen when I finally felt I was missing out on all the fun it looked like my best friends, Rose and Charlotte, were having smoking weed. So I smoked my first joint with Rosena, cleaning the reefer she'd taken from her sister's stash between the covers of an Earth, Wind & Fire album, then clumsily doing what she told me as I learned to roll it in Tops rolling papers.

Sometimes my sister Deb would come by and show up at Rose's bedroom door while we were rolling weed, singing songs, and smokin'. "What y'all doing?" she'd ask.

Rosena, ever the smart-mouthed jokester, would respond, "Get outta here, Fat Allen-Steamer! You can't come in here with us! You're too young and you tell everything!" Who knows where she came up with that nickname, but we'd all crack up laughing; Rose and I because we were high, and Deb because she is and was a good-natured sweetheart. She never got her feelings hurt. She knew Rose loved her, too, and making her leave was more to protect her at such a young age, from smoking, than anything else.

Charlotte, Rose, and I, all together or two of the three of us, spent a lot of hours smoking, singing, laughing, talking, and planning. We loved each other dearly and had so much fun enjoying each other's company this way. Little did we know then what this "fun" would lead to for one of us.

◆————————◎————————◆

Fact: Bullying is a very real problem for our children and too often can lead to drug or alcohol abuse. Tragically, it can sometimes end in suicide. Thousands of young people per year commit suicide and studies show that many of these cases are related to bullying.*

◆————————◎————————◆

Call to Action: When children report bullying, we must take these reports seriously and intervene. We must not make the victim feel guilty or weak.

Please see *Healing Waters: The Workbook* for an abundance of resources, conversation starters, and other ways to help children deal with bullying and ensure that they aren't the bullies!

*See endnote

Chapter 9

Can I Unsee This?

When dreams die, does what remains stink like a corpse?

*M*y thirteenth year opened the door to a hell that made seeing Troy end his life at my daddy's hand look like a Disney movie. This was the year Daddy was transferred from Stateville, the maximum security facility in Joliet. His good behavior, accomplishments, and many positive contributions to the facility brought him a lot of recognition. This earned him a move to a minimum security prison in the Vienna/Cairo area, in downstate Illinois.

When he moved downstate, he was afforded tremendous freedom. He enrolled in a program that trained him to become an EMT. He was able to work without constant supervision. After a short while, he only had to report back to the facility late in the evening to sleep. The setup was more like a halfway house than a prison. It was during this time that he met a woman we came to call "Thing." She worked with my dad as an emergency medical technician. Her given name was Ellen, but we saw her as a witch who came to destroy our dreams of having a normal family after so many years of waiting, praying, and planning. They began a hot and heavy affair and I can only imagine the conversations Daddy had with my mom about it.

My mother has never been one to give up easily, and I'm sure she felt strongly that she'd put too much time, money, energy, faith, and hope into my father and the life they would resume when he was released from prison to just let him go.

One weekend, she arranged for our grandparents and our Uncle E to look in on us and told us to go across the street to their house or upstairs to Uncle E's if we had any problems. Then she got into her old but well-kept car and headed south. I don't know everything that happened, but I do know that when she came home, she looked sad and defeated. Even so, she lovingly greeted us and fed us while she listened to tales of our weekend escapades. After she'd checked our homework and helped us lay our clothes out for the next day, we headed for bed.

Some time later, when I got up to go to the bathroom, I heard Mommy crying softly in her room. I knocked and went in to check on her. What she told me haunts me to this day. She said that when she got to Cairo, Thing was at his apartment. Daddy and this bitch sat on a couch together and Mom was forced to sit across from them in a chair. Mom cried and asked Daddy to come home. She asked him why he was doing this to her, to us. If she told me what his response was, I don't remember it. All I remember is her crying, literally sobbing out the details of the scene that had unfolded in front of her. She said the two of them started kissing and making out right in front of her! The more she begged him to stop, the heavier their petting got, and they even had sex in front of her! She told me that he said really nasty things to her while he said equally nasty things to Thing about the act they were engaged in.

She was crying uncontrollably now and all I could do was hold her as tight as I could while I added my sobs to hers. I didn't have words of comfort, not because I didn't want to comfort her, but because I was thirteen and had no clue what to say. All I know is that I felt undefinable pain and uncontrollable rage. It was in this moment that the unconditional love I'd always felt for my dad morphed into disgust and hate.

Sadly, the way the mind works, my mind anyway, turned my mom's words into graphic images that turned my stomach for years every time I thought of them. Eventually her sobs calmed to whimpers and at last she fell asleep in my arms. Not me, though. For me, sleep never came that night. I stayed up nursing the rage I felt toward my father and the sympathy I felt for my mother. I wondered how I could avenge her honor and take away her pain.

How did she do it?

Recently, I've driven to Memphis, Tennessee, about once a month for business. I've shed many tears for my mom as I've passed the exit signs to Cairo, Illinois. As I fly down the highway at eighty miles per hour in a new, comfortable car, my heart bleeds for the beautiful soul who would never hurt anyone, much less the man she loved through hell and stood faithfully by when most women would have cut their losses long before. Mommy drove home *alone,* in an old car with no air conditioning, in late spring when it was already hot. She probably relived the painful scene she'd just been subjected to by the man on whom she'd hung all her hopes and dreams for the last seven years and his whore. How did she see to drive through the tears that surely clouded her vision? How did she process the fact that the man she'd loved, waited for, and fought for through all those years was suddenly in the arms of another woman and she was left alone to continue raising three children? Did she think about what she'd say to us? About what she might say to all the "friends" and relatives who'd told her to divorce him and not wait for him when he was first convicted?

I don't know what she thought about or how she got through that fateful drive back to Rockford, but I do know that Ms. Amazing didn't give up. I do know that she didn't retaliate and respond with hatred or anger. I do know that she didn't take her pain out on us three children. I do know that she didn't turn to drugs or alcohol. She didn't quit her job, and she didn't stop being excellent at work or parenting. She continued being consistent and showing up in every way. She kept speaking life and kept praying. She was a ride-or-die wife long before the phrase gained popularity. Her strength, commitment, and resilience absolutely amaze me. Surely we are entertaining one of God's special angels.

It quickly became abundantly clear that what appeared to be two healthy adults working through a devastating experience to preserve their family was all a facade on Daddy's part. Mommy was the true glue, the strength, and the hero during all those years. Daddy's mask of love and appreciation for all my mom did for him while he was incarcerated was dropped. He was free now. Free from prison and free to "punish" my mom for her testimony and the lie he was told by his sister and sister-in-law about her fidelity.

My mom, though, wasn't ready to give up on her dream. She'd already spent years fighting for her husband, marriage, and family, so she took a breath, dug in, and resolved to keep fighting. I can't imagine how much it must have pained her to swallow her pride, to say whatever she said to persuade him to come home, but after a few awkward visits, he moved in with us. This was when the real chaos began. He immediately started hanging out at a house across the alley from us, where three or four men lived together. He'd cross the alley and hang out with them for hours, then return home drunk and belligerent.

Can I still be a princess if my king acts like a frog?

Who was this man who was completely turning our world upside down? Where was the daddy in whose eyes I had seen nothing but love and adoration? This man was nothing nice. He was verbally abusive and seemed to never have anything good to say to any of us. Sometimes he'd yell at us, drunkenly calling us names, or push one of us, daring us to hit him back. As much as I think I loved Daddy more strongly than my siblings did because of the time we'd shared bonding before his incarceration, I think my anger and unwillingness to let him bully us also outpaced theirs. I matched him word for word, calling him names and telling him he should just "get the fuck out."

I would gladly have physically fought him, but before I could, my sister and brother always intervened and begged me, "Just leave. Just go over grandmother's! We'll call you later." Then they'd literally push me out of the house, sometimes in the winter, wearing nothing but my T-shirt, shorts, and flip flops.

When I got across the street, I'd pace back and forth, fuming about what I was going to do to him while Lynn, Charlotte, and Shirley tried to calm me down and distract me with music or jokes. It usually didn't work because I was too upset, but they never gave up trying.

When Daddy finally passed out, one of my siblings would call to tell me it was okay for me to come back home. I tried many times to convince them that we could take him. The four of us, sober and strong, against him, drunk and slow, seemed like good odds to me, but they would have none of it.

With no outside intervention, Daddy and I stayed locked in a battle of wills. Our dislike for each other seeming to grow by the day, with my soul and self-esteem taking a beatdown that led to years of me tripping through one abusive relationship after another before I finally started to see the light through decades of prayer, therapy, and a lot of hard work.

Before long, he reached a new low when he brought Thing to Rockford and moved her into the house across the alley with the guys he regularly got drunk with. This was a major blow to all of us, the epitome of selfishness. This was the neighborhood we'd lived in for years. *Our* home, not his. *Our* family, friends, and neighbors, not his! He was a guest who should have been on his best behavior, but instead he crashed in like a Tasmanian devil, leaving tears and broken spirits in his wake.

Once again, Daddy's actions brought our family shame and embarrassment, but thankfully nobody teased us, bullied us, or tried to make us feel bad or responsible for his behavior. We were treated the same as before this new nightmare began.

Call to Action: We may not always be able to persuade our loved ones to leave an abusive situation, but we can provide support. We can remind them of their worth. We can offer to help shield or protect their children.

Please see *Healing Waters: The Workbook* for resources and tips to support loved ones in abusive situations.

Chapter 10

I Will Eff You Up!

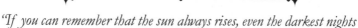

"If you can remember that the sun always rises, even the darkest nights become more bearable.," Angel Allen Townsend

Angry and exhausted

Many times on a school night, Daddy would wake us up to sing and dance with him. Even though Ma protested, he persisted, turning the music up and shouting for us to wake up and come dance with him. He thought this was normal and fun. He was totally oblivious to the fact that it was the middle of the night and we were young children who needed our rest to do well in school.

Sometimes we enjoyed these impromptu dance parties, but they often devolved into angry tirades and more abusive language. No matter how late we were made to stay up, though, Ma still insisted that we go to school.

One day when I was particularly exhausted, sad, and frustrated, I entered my eighth-grade French class, the class I took over Spanish because my mom studied French in school and I wanted to follow in her footsteps. I took my seat in the center of the room and promptly put my head down on my book to rest my mind. Before long, our teacher, Ms. Miller, called from the front of the room for me to sit up. I ignored her. I was so tired! A few minutes later, she called my name again. Again, I ignored her.

I guess this pissed her off because she walked to my desk and, standing over me, said, "Angel, I'm not going to tell you again; sit up and pay attention."

"I'm tired. Leave me alone," I responded.

"No. You can't sleep in my class." She nudged me as she spoke.

"Keep your hands offa me! I told you I don't feel good!" I still had my head down but I was aware that all eyes must have been on our exchange because the room was completely silent. I'm sure she saw my defiance as a test of wills and an affront to her authority. She had no intention of letting a little thirteen-year-old run her classroom, so she punched my arm harder this time and started to repeat her demand. Before she could finish her sentence, I'd jumped out of my seat, snatched up my heavy French book and slammed her in the face with it!

"Bitch, I told you not to put your hands on me again! I told you I don't feel good. Leave me the fuck alone!" She was holding her face and screaming, I'm sure as much from shock as pain.

"Get out of my classroom! You're going to the principal's office!"

"Fuck you!" I yelled back.

The room filled with oohs and ahhs as the other students laughed and pointed.

"She slapped the shit outta you!"

"Dayum!"

My favorite teacher, Mrs. Patterson, from my favorite subject and class, English, heard all the commotion from her classroom next door and was at my side like magic.

"Angel, calm down!" she said as she took me by my shoulders and made me look into her eyes. My eyes were wild and tear-filled. Hers were full of concern and calm.

"Get her outta here!" Ms. Miller said, still holding her face. Mrs. Patterson picked up my book with one hand and, putting her arm around me, led me out of the room and into hers. After the door was closed, she knelt next to me and held me while I sobbed. I couldn't get a word out to tell her what was going on at home, but she seemed to know I needed compassion, not punishment.

Somehow, I dodged a bullet that day. Mrs. Patterson pulled some strings and I wasn't even suspended, much less expelled like I probably should have been. I stayed in Ms. Miller's class and managed to stay awake for the rest of the year. I even got all the assignments in on time *and* earned a B for the semester. We kept our distance from each other, but I'm sure Mrs. Patterson told her that I was having problems at home and to go easy on me. Mrs. Patterson was my God-sent angel that day and I am forever grateful.

Please wake us when this nightmare is over

Daddy would drunkenly go between the house where Thing was staying and our house. He looked a hot mess most of the time and was anything but a father figure to us or a good husband to our mom. Every so often, Daddy would attempt sobriety. Even while he was sober, he wasn't good for or to our mom. He still openly saw Thing, and sadly my mother endured it. At the time, I didn't understand why she stayed because all I could see was how much his presence and actions were hurting all of us.

I know now that she is really that woman who loves unconditionally and lives out 1 Corinthians 13:4–8. I see now that she is one of the strongest women I've ever known. I understand now, as an adult, that sometimes leaving is easy and staying, believing, praying, and fighting for family takes courage, faith, and strength. I know that each person has to find their own way and do what they believe is best for them and their families. Today I understand, respect, and appreciate my mom in a way I didn't as a child. I can only imagine the turmoil she must have felt, the prayers she must have prayed, and the begging she must have done to get my dad to keep all the promises he had made to her and to us while he was locked down. Does she give up on her dream of again being a loving, healthy family—two people in love; raising beautiful, successful, well-adjusted children; enjoying the fruits of their labor, grandchildren, and growing lovingly old together? If that was all she had ever dreamed, all she had ever imagined, and I'm absolutely sure it was, what would she have if she gave that up? How could she, once again, create a new normal?

Daddy would actually get all cleaned up on Friday. He'd shower, shave, apply "smell-good," and then pack a small bag, all while we watched and were fully aware of what he was doing. He was preparing to spend the weekend with Thing! Wow! He'd then return Sunday night and resume his position, business as usual, on the sofa, watching TV, reading the paper, maybe cooking a meal or two. This all happened *while he was attempting sobriety!*

One Sunday night, he returned home and came into the room my sister and I shared. Our room was separated by a door from our parents' room (I know, odd setup—our home was a former funeral home, so the layout was strange). He stood there, laughing and talking with us, asking us how our weekend had been, acting like this arrangement was normal! I know our mom, who was in their room, could hear him talking, but she's never been confrontational, nor did she want to argue with him in front of her children, so she remained quiet. Daddy seemed to get louder, laughing at nothing and talking about even less. I couldn't help but wonder what she must be feeling. How was she dealing with the fact that he'd been gone all weekend and was now hanging out with us kids instead of at least checking on her?

The conversation was fake and hollow and I was squirming with anger, sadness, and extreme discomfort the whole time. Why was he even in here? It wasn't like we had called out to him. We certainly hadn't missed him over the weekend. It was just the opposite; why had he come back at all? To rub his disrespect for us in our faces? How could he not be concerned about our mom's feelings? About our thoughts and feelings? About not further injuring our tender minds, hearts, and perspective of relationships, marriage, fidelity, and sex?

I was embarrassed and angry at both of them! Why did Mommy take it and subject us to this madness? Why didn't Daddy just leave if he was so miserable with us? Where was this all headed? When would it end?

Every now and then, though, I'd peep glimpses of Daddy's true heart, the heart of love that was calloused over by years of trauma and pain.

Once a young man, Ralph, was supposed to pick me up to take me bowling with some of our other friends. Our families knew each other from church and I was looking forward to going out for a fun, relaxing time. I was all dressed, waiting patiently and excitedly for him to show up. I waited, and waited, and waited. Both my parents were home and we were having a rare decent conversation. The longer I waited, the angrier Daddy got.

Eventually he said, "No boy has the right to treat my angel like this! Even if he comes now, you can't go! This is disrespectful! We're taking you out!"

Almost on cue, Ralph called to say he was on his way.

Daddy took the phone from me and said, "Nah, man, not tonight. You're two hours late. Why you just now calling?"

I don't know what Ralph's response was, but Daddy hung up the phone, kissed me on my forehead, and went to change his clothes. Mommy changed hers, too, and the three of us went out for a dinner that made me hope again. The irony here is that Daddy's typical behavior taught me very well to accept disrespect and dishonor. This gesture was just that, a gesture, a fond memory and a reminder of my dying dreams.

Young, stupid love

A couple of months later, I was at a friend's house when her brother walked in with his friend LT, who was on the basketball team at one of the local high schools. Because of his incredible height— seven foot one—he was well known to just about everyone in town. So, while I'd heard of him and seen him around, I'd never met him. When he walked in, I was nice, but not particularly interested in him. I got more interested when LT and my friend's brother told us they had weed and asked us if we wanted to smoke. That was the first of many days the four of us spent together, laughing, smoking, and just hanging out.

One evening after we'd been hanging out for several hours, LT offered to take me home so I wouldn't have to walk by myself. I accepted and we exchanged numbers before I got out of his car. He called me the same night and we ended up talking for hours. Before I knew it, we were dating. The two of us started to spend as much time together as we did with our friends who introduced us.

I was just fourteen when I met LT and barely fifteen when we started dating. He took me to his house to meet his mom, Mary, who was dismissive and not very friendly. I figured she just didn't know me yet and I committed to trying to win her over. Whenever I visited, I offered to help cook or clean up the kitchen. She readily accepted, but it seemed that the first day I met her, she was on her best behavior because she only became more unpleasant, condescending, and disrespectful. I don't remember her ever being genuinely nice.

Her nasty attitude wasn't enough to keep me from her son, though. We were getting closer and before long, we were professing our love for each other. He immediately started pressuring me for sex. I didn't feel ready and I was scared to death, but I didn't want to lose him and I let myself be convinced that "if I really loved him, I'd show him by letting him make love to me."

Lord, why didn't anybody tell me what a horrible experience that would be?! We'd smoked plenty of weed beforehand, but the unexpected, searing pain completely blew my high! As unpleasant as it was, losing my virginity to LT cushioned a blow that I had no idea was soon to come.

Anyway, I began spending the night with LT on a regular basis. I just told my parents that I was staying with a friend. Daddy was too drunk to care and Mommy trusted that I was making sound decisions and usually believed what I told her. LT's mom indulged her son ridiculously. She allowed me—at fifteen!—to spend the night with her nineteen-year-old son anytime he wanted me to stay.

Call to Action: I can't emphasize enough how important it is to meet the parents of your children's boyfriends and girlfriends. Mary might have still been the abusive, unpleasant person that she was, but meeting my mother might have made her think twice before she continually disrespected me or let a child spend the night in her house, smoking weed and having sex with her grown son.

Chapter 11

More Heartbreak

"Learn not to fear death, for we are energy and energy is. Death transforms energy, it doesn't end it." Angel Allen Townsend

I continued to smoke weed regularly with Rosena and my other friends and cousins. I had four male cousins, David, Philip, Barry, and Craig, whom I hung out with all the time! They loved and protected me. We smoked, joked, laughed, and talked about our futures. They were positive male figures in my life and they brought joy and comfort to many dreary days.

I was becoming increasingly concerned about Rose, though. I knew who she was hanging out with more and I knew they were experimenting with other drugs. There'd be times when I was sitting in the car with my boyfriend, LT late at night and she'd come stumbling down the street, clearly very high on something more than weed. I'd hop out of the car and make sure she got into her house okay, then sit with her at their kitchen table or up in her room, asking her what she was getting herself into and begging her to stop it, whatever it was. She'd usually chuckle, telling me I worried too much and she was fine. I'd help her get in bed if her sister wasn't home, then rejoin LT in his car if he'd waited or go inside my own house to crawl into bed.

Early one December morning, our phone rang. It was Charlotte. She was crying. "What's wrong?" I asked, not too concerned. Even though we were fifteen and Lynn was seventeen, they still got into it periodically. I thought she was calling to complain about something mean Lynn had done to her. "What did Lynn do to you now?"

She didn't answer. She just cried harder.

Now I was panicked. "What's wrong, Charlotte?! You're scaring me!"

"Rose died," she choked out.

"*What?* What did you say?!"

"Rosena, she died . . ." She was sobbing loudly now.

"No, that's impossible!" I shouted into the phone. "I was just with her yesterday! I'm calling her now!"

I pressed the hook to hang up the phone, then called Rosena's house. Her dad answered.

"Hey T.D., can I speak to Rose?" I said, trying to sound normal as I tasted the fear in the back of my throat.

"Rose is dead," he said with what sounded like no emotion.

"No!" I let out a bloodcurdling scream, dropped the phone, and fell to my knees.

Mommy was immediately at my side. "Angel! What's wrong?" she asked as she picked up the phone.

"Hello? Who's this? Thomas? What happened?"

"Rose died last night. I gotta go," he said to my mom as he hung up the phone.

The days leading up to my best friend's funeral were a blur. Everybody at school knew we were best friends and our house phone rang off the hook with nosy questions from people who'd long ago written Rose off as someone who got high and skipped school. Still, in our neighborhood, she was deeply loved. She was one of us and we fiercely protected our own.

My answers were short and curt. "Why do you care? You weren't her friend. Why are you calling now?" I said before I slammed the phone down yet again.

It turns out that another neighborhood girl's aunt died and sent her belongings to their house. She and Rose went through the aunt's stuff and found pills that turned out to be methadone, the drug used to help heroin addicts get clean. They probably took too many and drank alcohol. The next morning, when the other girl went to wake Rose up for breakfast, she was gone.

Rose was the friend I'd known and loved for most of my short but painful life. The friend I'd shared too many secrets with to count. The friend who'd comforted me when I cried about my crazy daddy. The friend I'd become blood sisters with all those years before when she, Charlotte, and I sat in her room, smushing our pricked fingers together and vowing to always have each other's backs. In the blink of an eye, my best friend was gone.

Her funeral was nearly unbearable. Aretha Franklin's beautiful voice filled the space as "Precious Memories" played on a continuous loop. The room was packed with spectators more than mourners, which pissed me off, but I couldn't worry about that. I was there to say goodbye to my sister.

"Are you sure you're up for this?" my mom asked me.

"Yeah, I need to see her," I responded.

My mom half-carried me to the front of the room to gaze into my friend's peaceful, beautiful face. The minute I got close enough to see that it was her, I passed out. When I came to, I was sitting on the front bench, my mom fanning me and rubbing my hands. I cried like I'd lost my best friend because I had. It wasn't just me, though. All our neighborhood friends were crying just as hard, some running from the room, some standing, wringing their hands in disbelief. Rose's family sat on a front bench, holding each other and crying, too.

Finally, I worked up the nerve to look at her. She did look like my regular Rose, like a sleeping beauty. My mom held me up while I whispered my goodbyes and kissed her cheek for the last time.

I miss her, still.

It's hard to explain
I'm never gonna see you again
And you'll never meet my new friends

Sade, "Maureen"

It seems Rose's death left our entire neighborhood reeling. In an attempt to make sense of the senseless, we looked harshly toward the girl she was with. We knew it wasn't her fault, but we just wanted answers. Answers she, of course, didn't have. She, too, had lost a dear friend. She had found Rose unresponsive and carried the heavy burden of guilt, mostly alone. From appearances, this took a tremendous toll on her and I pray she has forgiven herself and found peace.

Adding to our neighborhood family's pain, Rose's older sister, Thomasina, met a tragic ending when only four years later she was found beaten and strangled on a freezing December night, her young body dumped on the side of the road.

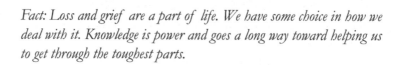

Fact: Loss and grief are a part of life. We have some choice in how we deal with it. Knowledge is power and goes a long way toward helping us to get through the toughest parts.

Call to Action: When a loved one experiences loss, please pay attention to their behaviors. Check in with them. Conversation isn't always necessary. Sometimes the best support is to be present and available to them.

Please see *Healing Waters: The Workbook* for the stages of grief and resources on dealing with grief, signs to look for, and how young people may deal differently with grief and loss.

Chapter 12

Same Madness, Different House

————————

"If you wanted to look better in print, you should have acted better in life." Angel Allen Townsend

I walked around in a daze for months after Rose died. I barely ate and partied harder than ever. I hung out with people who smoked weed like I did. I drank, too, but my drug of choice, by far, was weed. Thank God for that! With my daddy's alcoholism and my propensity to anesthetize, I could have easily become hooked on something else or ended up like Rose.

I kept going to school, though, because I believed that would be my way out of Rockford, the place that seemed to hold nothing but pain for me.

Even though I was only fifteen, I also found a job. I lied about my age and applied at Montgomery Ward, a department store two bus rides away from our house. I got the job and was assigned to work in the candy department with Bea.

Bea was a no-nonsense woman who happened to live up the street from us. Her girls were part of our neighborhood crew and I already knew her well. She, like so many of the other adults in our neighborhood, was like an aunt to me. She already knew everything that was going on with our family and was yet another angel that God gave me to speak life into and over me, to encourage me and listen to me when I was hurting. She reminded me that I was special and could do anything I set my mind to. She wasn't a softy, though. She made sure I did my job well and didn't hesitate to tell me if I did something wrong or she thought I was slacking. She showed me how to do something once, maybe twice, then expected me to duplicate her actions, and 98 percent of the time, I did. I caught on quickly, learning how to make the ice cream and Icees and clean the machines afterward, measure the candy, fill the candy bins, take orders, and work the cash register.

Fortunately, I was good with numbers at a time when the register didn't tell how much change to give back; the cashier had to figure it out for themselves and I was trusted with handling the money part of the job right away. I loved that job and I loved being around Bea. I took as many hours as I could while still getting to school. Bea was truly another shelter from the storm I called my life. As I look back over my life, I see that God provided me angels along the way to keep me going, keep me safe, or snatch me back from the jaws of death or mental breakdown.

Weebles wobble, but they don't fall down

In the midst of all this, my mom's mother, who'd been diagnosed with early onset dementia a few years earlier, began to need even more assistance. My mom, Deb, and I began to bathe her, shampoo and braid her hair, and take care of all her other daily hygiene, meal prep, and care needs. My grandfather was there, but he left most of the care of his wife to the three of us. My brother also stepped right up and did all he could. When my grandfather wasn't home, one of the four of us stayed with my grandmother. A few other family members popped in to offer assistance every now and then, and grandfather hired a part-time caretaker until our grandmother got to the point when she needed more full-time care than all of us combined could provide. Then my grandfather reluctantly placed her in a nursing home for the final months of her life.

Never once did I hear my mom complain about adding the new daily task of taking care of her mom to her already full plate. She didn't seem to question for one minute that this was the right and honorable thing to do. Her sister and her family lived in Chicago and although both her brothers and their families lived in town, they had their hands full with their lives. Uncle Al was battling cancer and James was—well, who knows what he was doing? I just know he wasn't around. Not only did she not question their absence, but she never showed anything other than the same love and affection toward each of them that she always had. This scenario played itself out again when several years later my grandfather moved into our family home after he collapsed in his kitchen from a then unknown illness. This amazing woman took her dad in, fed him, and took care of his finances and anything else he needed until the day he transitioned. My sister and I were away at college by this time, so my brother jumped in and cleaned out our grandparents' house to prepare it for sale.

And still, it looked like our daddy drama wasn't going to end anytime soon. Mommy not only kept putting up with his nonsense and abuse, but she dug in deeper. About six months after Rose passed, our parents told us we were moving across town to a new house. I don't know if Mommy made it happen by herself or if Daddy played a part in the purchase of the first home they'd ever owned or the new car we got around the same time, but I wasn't unhappy to be leaving our old neighborhood. There was so much pain there. Rose was gone and seeing her house every day was a stabbing reminder of her absence. Thing still lived across the alley and not having to see her ugly, wrinkled face was a welcome relief.

Life hits us with another blow

Before we could move into our new house, my mother's beloved older brother, who'd been battling prostate cancer for five years, died at only forty years old. We'd spent so much time at their house over the years, especially during daddy's incarceration. My mom was extremely close to Uncle Al and his sweetheart of a wife, Aunt Pat. Our three cousins were older than we were, but they tolerated us well and let us hang out with them when we came over. My mom's taking us over there so regularly helped us to build relationships with our cousins that still thrive today. She made sure she surrounded us with people who would love us unconditionally, like she had inner knowledge about what we needed to help us play the rough hand we'd been dealt. When Uncle Al passed, I could tell it knocked the wind out of Mommy's sails, at least for a minute. With everything that was going on with Daddy and the new house, she barely had time to grieve, but for several months after he died, she didn't laugh or smile as regularly and she was much more reserved than usual.

Daddy's drama continues

I guess it was good that we had the new house to distract us a bit. It had three bedrooms on the first floor, one for each of us. This was special for all of us; each of us children got our own room and privacy! The second floor of the house was one huge room that spanned the length of the house. There was also a large walk-in closet. This was my parents' room. Things started out well enough. Daddy was again attempting sobriety and we all seemed to be trying hard to make our family work. Daddy seemed to have a hard time getting a decent job. I'm sure this was in large part due to the X on his back, courtesy of what we now know as the Prison Industrial Complex. This evil system is designed to keep ex-felons from regaining full citizenship after their release from prison.

I imagine that phrase "X on his back" signified a lot when it was coined. What does an X do? It crosses out or eliminates something or someone. It invalidates that thing. It indicates a lack of worthiness or value. It says, "Don't touch," "Don't buy," "Don't hire." It effectively separates that something from the rest. It destroys self-esteem, opportunities, families, and communities.

We must continue to work to change the laws governing the penal system. Once a person has successfully served their sentence, they should be allowed to wholly reintegrate into society. That person should be afforded the same rights and privileges as anybody else, including voting, running for office, and becoming gainfully employed. Anything less encourages engagement in criminal activity and risk of re-incarceration, causes depression, and leads to further destruction of families as well as drug or alcohol abuse. These archaic laws negatively impact us all. As a society, we all suffer a returning citizen's ongoing and, too often, racially biased "punishment." Of course, I'm not making a sweeping statement or speaking of hardened criminals, at large. That is a bigger conversation for another book. If you're interested in learning more about how the criminal "injustice" system, by design, strips shocking numbers of black and brown people of their rights, several excellent books cover the subject in depth. One I highly recommend is *The New Jim Crow* by Michelle Alexander.

(As of the writing of this book, most states do not allow persons who are imprisoned, in jail awaiting trial, or on parole to vote. When we take into account how many people languish in jail awaiting trial because they cannot afford bail, how many are imprisoned for petty crimes, and how many are re-incarcerated because of equally petty crimes, the numbers of those systematically removed from the voting rolls is frighteningly staggering. This alone should be a call to action for all of us. The right to vote is just that: a right hard-won for the majority of Americans. Losing this right shouldn't be taken lightly.)*

When Daddy wasn't drinking, he was always fastidiously clean and neat. He kept the house in order and he and I shared a love of houseplants. We'd decide where to place each one after potting them together. We'd water them together and spend the time talking. Other times, if he was between jobs, he'd sit on the sofa, reading a book or scouring the paper for work.

Life, for a while, was quiet and normal. It was an all-too-short glimpse into what our family could have, should have, looked like. Even though Daddy seemed to be okay, there was always a slight restlessness about him.

This makes sense—who doesn't want to contribute to society, to the well-being of their family? Taking care of a grown, able-bodied person does both the caregiver and the recipient a grave disservice and nobody wins. It exhausts the caregiver, gives them too much control and misplaced power, and clips the wings of the recipient, causing resentment all around and enabling unhealthy behavior.

We served that time with you! We're hurting, too!

Mommy was out working every day, making it happen, holding down our entire family, just as she always had. I'm sure she was praying fervently for things to work out, too. In the movie, 'Bad Company', Ellen Barkin's character asks Laurence Fishburne's character if he knows why she hates their boss so much. Fishburne replies, "Probably because you owe him too much. Your only choices are hate and gratitude. Who wants to be grateful?" That certainly seemed to be the case between my parents. This lopsided dynamic gave Daddy an excuse to quickly resume drinking.

There's a parable in the Bible that speaks about removing a demon. If that demon comes back and finds the "house" swept clean and still empty, it moves back in, this time bringing several more demons with it (Luke 11:25). So, Daddy's drinking just seemed to escalate. He not only continued his shenanigans with Thing, but also started seeing other prostitutes. More than once, we were told that Daddy was seen in the passenger seat of our car with some woman driving. This was after he'd take Mommy to work. He'd go get some trick, get drunk, and then, with total disregard for his family, ride around town like he was single and childless and had purchased the car he was letting some ho drive!

Where he was in his alcohol-fueled, resentment-motivated, and traumatized illness is hard to understand. I've often wondered and later asked, did he not ever consider the possibility of his children, our friends, or other family members seeing them? Did he never, even while sober, consider how painful this could be? That our tender young minds and his loving, devoted wife had been traumatized enough already and his behavior was akin to snatching scabs off wounds again and again before they'd had time to heal? From the perspective of a child, this callous, irresponsible behavior is impossible to understand. From my perspective as an adult, I realize that mental illness is difficult to understand or explain and the best answer is to interrupt destructive behaviors borne of abuse and trauma to hopefully prevent untold damage to the individual, their family, and society.

What if the penal system included family therapy, free of charge and available for the asking, for all returning citizens? Or, even better, what if it was a required part of the parole program? What if our parents had received marital counseling to help them deal with their fears, misunderstandings, and misguided resentments? What if Daddy had re-entry classes available to him before he was released? What if we'd all taken classes to learn to communicate effectively—honestly and respectfully—with each other? What if...?

Fact: Coping and communication skills are just that: skills. Skills can be learned and require practice. Once coping and communication skills are employed, they can help save marriages, families, and communities.

Call to Action: The importance of open and honest communication can't be overstated when a family is in crisis, such as after a job loss. Practice considering the outcome you want before you start a conversation. If you want peace and reconciliation, don't start with yelling or accusations.

Please see *Healing Waters: The Workbook* for many tips, exercises, and ideas on how to start and continue difficult but necessary conversations in healthy and productive ways.

Call to Action: Regarding the Prison Industrial Complex and the School-to-Prison Pipeline—get involved. Call your congresspersons. Participate in your church's prison ministry. If it doesn't have one, consider starting one. Educate yourself by reading books like *The New Jim Crow* by Michelle Alexander, *Inside This Place, Not of It* edited by Ayelet Waldman and Robin Levi, *Chokehold, Policing Black Men,* by Paul Butler *or Understanding Mass Incarceration* by James Kilgore. These are just a few of the many books available.

*See endnote

Chapter 13

Cruel and Unusual Punishment

"Fathers, do not embitter your children or they will become discouraged"
(Colossians 3:21).

There were days when Daddy drank all day. He'd wake up drinking and was often drunk before we left for school. I'd always suffered from really horrible periods that kept me sick and out of school sometimes.

Once when I was home sick, Daddy was upstairs in the bed, probably drinking. The phone rang and he answered it. After a while I went to the bottom of the steps to see if it was Mommy or somebody else I might want to speak to. I listened for a minute and could tell he wasn't speaking to a family member or friend. Now, I was completely in "I don't trust you or respect you" mode, so I quietly picked up the extension to see who he was talking to. It was that nasty-ass Thing and they were having phone sex!

"Do you want my dick in your mouth?" Daddy asked her.

"Yeah," she responded.

"Then say it," he said.

"I want your dick in my mouth. I wanna suck your dick," she said quietly.

"Yeah, tell me more, bitch. What else do you want?"

Oh, my goodness! This asshole was yet again disrespecting my Mommy and us! He knew I was home sick, yet he chose to ignore the fact that I might overhear him and indulge his own selfish whims! I slammed the phone down on the hook, knowing he'd hear me. How could he?

He did this without so much as a thought for my sanity, in the house his entire family lived in, in the bed he shared most nights with my mother, in the house my Mommy's hard work made possible! Damn! Another memory my young mind didn't need to absorb! Another assault to my senses! Another blow to my self-esteem and another reason to feel a need to protect my mother from this monster. I was too young to be Mommy's defender and protector. Who was gonna defend and protect me? My mom never once made me feel like I needed to defend or protect her, but as the oldest and probably meanest and most outspoken, I misguidedly took it upon myself to do that as much as I could. I didn't tell her until years later what I'd heard. Why? It would have only been another blow she'd have to absorb and I really didn't think she'd leave him anyway, so why hurt her further? She knew her husband wasn't shit.

I may not have wanted to say anything to my mom, but I had to do *something* with all that hurt and anger I had bottled up inside. Every time Daddy looked at any one of us "wrong," I took it as a personal affront and challenged him. Our fights and arguments escalated to a shamefully disrespectful level. We cursed and yelled at each other like two enemies in the street would. He called me bitch, ho, slut, and whatever else he could think of. I hit back just as hard, calling him names and telling him he was a no-good dirty dog, not worthy to be in our lives and definitely not worthy of Mommy's love.

"Fuck you! You ain't shit!" I said during one of our many fights.

For whatever reason, this time he responded by picking up a wooden statue and throwing it at me with what seemed like all his strength. By God's grace, I ducked just in time and the statue crashed into the wall behind me, sending a shower of plaster to the floor and leaving a two-inch gaping hole where it made contact. This was a new low. Somehow, knowing my beloved daddy was willing to actually do me bodily harm hit me in my heart and soul. I burst out crying and ran to my room. My daddy, in his drunken, angry state, let me go. After a few minutes, my mom knocked softly on my door, then entered to hold me while I cried.

"Why don't you just leave him?" I wailed. "I hate him!"

"He doesn't hate you, honey," she replied. "He's just hurting and doesn't know how to get around it. He does need help. He's your daddy and we love him. Let's pray and see if we can help him get the help he needs."

Damn, she was so loving and *way too* forgiving. When do you cut bait for the sake of your children? I just lay in her arms for a while and, once again, we sat in silence, lost in our own thoughts.

That hole stayed in the wall for years. It was a constant reminder of the broken place we all lived in as a result of the interruption to our lives years earlier, with no healing work done to offset that seismic shift.

I'm punch drunk, don't know how many more blows I can take . . .

I'd always loved music and spent many afternoons after school and Saturdays at the record store, Ubiquity Records, up the street from us. Sonny and Cherry Crudup let me hang out there for hours, laughing, talking, and listening to the newest hits. This was where I happily spent most of my allowance. I'd run home with my latest treasure and head straight to my room to play my new (and old) records over and over. Music allowed me to escape my pain—first because I missed my daddy, and later when I hated that he was home. I had quite a collection and it was my prized possession. I didn't let anyone play my albums! If somebody wanted to hear a record, they had to wait until I got home and only I could put the record on the turntable. I didn't want to take a chance on them getting scratched.

One day as I walked the few blocks home from the bus stop, I noticed albums strewn along the sidewalk.

Hmm, I thought, who lost their albums? That's too bad.

As I kept walking, I saw more and more, some in the street, some on neighbors' porches. Curiosity got the best of me and I picked one up. I saw *my* handwriting, in the way I wrote on every album, with my name and the date I'd purchased it!

My head started spinning! "What could this mean?!"

I walked a few steps and picked up another one. Same thing. This was mine, too. Now I really started to panic! I started running toward home, picking up albums as I went. There were so many, and they were all mine! I picked up as many as I could carry, then ran the rest of the way home. I burst into the house.

"Hello? Is anybody home?" I shouted.

No answer. I ran to my room to confirm what I already knew. I was shook by the sight of the empty crates that used to hold my beloved collection. I brushed away the tears that stung my eyes. I didn't have time to cry; I had to go get my albums! I ran back outside, picking up albums as I went. Many covers were empty and many albums lay broken on the street. When I got back home, I'd recovered less than a third of my collection.

Yes, I was angry, angry enough to chew knives, but I was more hurt. I was so hurt! It felt like every cell in my body was on fire from the pain of feeling like my daddy surely must hate me to hit me so hard, in a way that he knew would cut me to the core! This act of violence couldn't be dismissed by alcoholism; it was too deliberate. How could he take the one thing he knew I loved, where I found peace, and destroy it?

By late afternoon, my mom, sister, and brother were home. Deb and Dean looked sorry for me as I cried about my loss and my mom was shocked into silence. Daddy walked in, drunk as usual, a short time later and just looked at me, eyes half-closed from drunkenness. He smoked his cigarette as I cried, begging him to tell me why he hated me so much and why he wanted to hurt me.

Once again, my mom tried to comfort me. She could hold me and wipe my tears, but she couldn't explain away or protect me from his brutal acts of emotional and psychological violence. Years later, Daddy apologized and tried to explain that he was in the throes of the disease of alcoholism. I forgave him and we moved on with rebuilding our relationship, but the damage was considerable and lingered for years.

Gremlins just won't quit

LT and I got even closer. I just wanted to be away from home as much as possible, so I was at his house a lot. His mother was still abusive to me. She ridiculed me every chance she got and LT never took up for me. She condoned his seeing other girls at the same time he was dating me.

One Christmas I came over to have breakfast and open gifts. When I reached for the wrong one, I saw that it had his other girlfriend's name on it.

"Oh, that's not yours. That one is for Kayla," she said with what sounded like glee in her voice. "She'll be here shortly, so as soon as you open yours, you need to leave." Devil's spawn.

LT's weak behind just sat there and let her talk to me like that. In my brokenness I actually thought I had the better deal. At least I got to have breakfast with this evil cabal. Kayla just got to come over to open her gifts. Mommy and Daddy's unspoken lessons were taking hold very well and I didn't even realize it.

Fact: I was clearly negatively impacted by my father's alcohol addiction. I'm sure I would have benefited from talking to someone.

Call to Action: If you have or had a drug- or alcohol-addicted parent or other influential adult in the home, look into programs like Al-Anon and Alateen. These programs help families and friends of alcoholics to cope, understand, and recover.

Chapter 14

People: Some Good, Some Really Bad

Trauma, trauma everywhere!

Somehow, about three months into my employment at Montgomery Ward, the human resources department found out that I was about six months from being a legal hire. They loved me so much, they told me that even though they couldn't allow me to stay, as soon as I turned sixteen, my job would be waiting for me. Before I was put on hiatus, though, I met a new demon sent to deliver another soul blow. A guy named Skip who worked in the electronics department at Ward's stopped by the candy department to talk to Bea and he often brought his brother Chuck with him. Skip was nice and "normal." His brother, on the other hand, seemed odd. He was quiet but his eyes looked sinister, like he was up to no good. He began to engage me while his brother joked with Bea.

It started innocently enough. "Do you like working here?" he asked. "Are you still in school? Planning to go to college?"

As I began to warm up to him, his conversation slowly became less innocent and more predatory.

"Don't eat too much of that candy; you don't want to mess up that perfect figure!"

"You are sooo cute! I bet all the guys love you!"

His plan was insidious. I didn't realize he was going in for the kill and I was easy prey until it was too late. I appreciated the attention from an older man. He bolstered my fragile ego. From the abuse I was getting from my dad at home to the confirmation of that abuse by LT and his mom, I was ripe for the picking.

Before I left Ward's and for many months during the hiatus, I began to visit Chuck at his apartment. I never really had to explain my whereabouts to my parents. They were too distracted with their own drama to notice I was missing. Almost immediately, Chuck made it very clear that I was really just prey; I was there for sex only and any relationship beyond sex wasn't happening. Chuck was in his late thirties and I was barely a teenager who'd only recently lost my virginity to a guy who fooled me into thinking he loved me.

The first time we arrived at Chuck's apartment, the door was barely closed behind me when I realized I'd entered hell.

"So, you wanna have a bowl of ice cream first or do you wanna fuck, then have ice cream?" he asked.

I must have looked at him like I'd been punched in the face because he said, "What? I remember what you told me. I know how much you like ice cream, so I got you some. You know we're fucking tonight, right? So, what? Ice cream first?"

I was shocked and scared. I didn't know how I was gonna get out of there.

I didn't know what to do. I don't know why, but I stammered, "Um, ice cream, I guess." He got me a bowl of ice cream and handed it to me. He got undressed as he watched me eat it. Tears rolled down my cheeks as I ate the ice cream as slowly as I could. I was sick to my stomach, but I felt there was no way I could escape this monster.

At one point, he said, "Hurry up! What's taking you so long? I need to get your ass back home soon. I gotta go to work in the morning!"

When I finally finished my ice cream, he took the bowl out of my hand and told me to go to the bedroom. He instructed me to get undressed and get under the covers. As crazy as it sounds, I took my barely more than a baby behind into the bedroom and did exactly as I was told.

He came in, climbed on top of me and raped me without one word between us. When he finished, he got up and told me to go clean myself up so he could get me home. On the drive to my house,

I looked out the window and whimpered quietly, shocked by what had just happened.

He seemed almost giddy as he talked about how "young and sweet and juicy" I was and how he couldn't wait for us to get together again. I couldn't respond, knowing that my voice would break from painful emotion if I tried. When we got to my house, as I opened the door and moved to step out of the car, he said, "I'll call soon so we can get together again! That was your favorite ice cream, right?"

He squeezed my butt as I wordlessly stepped out of the car without so much as a glance back at him. He chuckled as I closed the door and pulled away before I'd taken two steps.

A life out of control

A preferred ending to this story would be that I reported the rape and that he was arrested, convicted and imprisoned for violating me the way he did that night. That would have been justice, but that's not what happened. Instead, I went inside, hiding my tears and my shame. Fortunately, it was late, and everyone was in bed for a change. I took a two-hour bath, attempting to scrub the shame and pain away. I cried myself to sleep that night. In the morning, I pulled myself together, and I never told.

I wish I could say that was the only time we got together, but this scenario played itself out many times over the next few months. I went from LT's bed to Chuck's and back again. I wish I could say I understood why I accepted endless abuse from both of these men, LT's mother, and my dad, all at the same time. I wish I could say why I didn't find the courage to tell my mom what was going on so maybe she could help me. I guess I didn't think my mother could help me; she was on the receiving end of her own massive abuse.

I guess one good thing was that from the age of eleven, when I first started my period, I was on the pill. My periods were so excruciatingly painful, the doctor said the only way to give me some relief was to start me on birth control pills. I was so embarrassed to be on the pill at such a young age. That was something older girls or women did! I wasn't ready to be on the pill! I was still a little girl and wanted so badly to be just that and only that.

Anyway, since I was being passed between two grown men who never even considered condoms and I was too naive, too damaged, too broken to mention it, the pill was probably what saved me from an unwanted pregnancy.

It couldn't save me from a sexually transmitted disease, though. After several weeks of this nightmare, I began to have really bad stomach cramps that were unaccompanied by my period. I also had a funky discharge. When it wasn't going away, I got scared and told my mom. She didn't say much, just looked at me kinda sadly and said she'd make me a doctor's appointment so we could see what was going on.

She went with me to the doctor, but wasn't in the room with me during the exam. After the pap smear and full exam, the doctor asked me a lot of questions that were really embarrassing.

"When did you start having sex?"

"About six months ago."

"Are you having sex with more than one person?"

"Yes, two guys."

"Are they having sex with other people?"

"I don't know, but I think they are, yes."

"Are you having unprotected sex?"

My head dropped in total sadness and shame. "Yes," I said.

"Do your parents know about this?'

"I don't know. I don't think so. I didn't tell them."

"Well, Angel, how much do you know about sexually transmitted diseases?"

"Not much, only what I learned in school. Why?"

"Because I have to inform you that you have one. You have gonorrhea."

"What?! Oh, my God! Can I be cured? Are you gonna tell my mother? Please don't tell her! She'll be so mad at me!"

"Yes, we have to tell her because of your age. You can be cured. We're gonna give you penicillin shots that'll take care of it, but if you plan to continue having sex, you have to use protection. This is serious! You can't play with your health!"

The doctor called my mom back into the room and told her the same thing he'd just told me.

She hugged me tight, tears flowing down her face, and whispered, "I'm so sorry, honey. I love you."

Then she told me she'd wait for me in the waiting room to take me home. After she left, the doctor told me that the shots would hurt a bit and that I shouldn't have sex for at least two weeks and definitely not at all without my partner wearing a condom.

The nurse held my hand while he gave me a shot in each buttock that felt like fire. I got dressed and went out into the waiting room to meet my mom.

"Mommy, they gave me two shots!" I announced loudly.

God, even with all I'd seen and been through in my fifteen short years, I was still such a little girl! My mom looked embarrassed and grabbed my hand, shushing me as she pulled me toward the elevator.

Sadly, we never spoke of it again. I was left to digest, process, and figure out how to move forward on my own. I didn't do well on any of those fronts.

I was angry and rebellious at the doctor for telling my mom when I'd asked him not to. As young and naive as I was, I believed I was grown enough to handle myself and I was stubborn.

Boy, was I stubborn. I felt so strongly that I could take care of myself and that I had to prove that to everyone, starting with the doctor. I sadly went and got myself infected again. I went back to that same doctor, on my own this time, and told him to treat me without telling my mom. My fifteen-year-old dumb ass thought this was a sane approach. I didn't even confront either man about the infection. To this day, I think I know who the culprit was (that nasty-ass pedophile Chuck). but I never got confirmation of that from either of them.

I'm sure that doctor thought I was crazy and my family was totally dysfunctional. I never thought about how my actions might have affected my mom. She was, after all, a nurse in this hospital and probably had a working relationship with this doctor. In retrospect, I'm sure he told her I'd been back in. Did he ask her not to mention it to me? He must have because she never did. I can only imagine and thank God now for how much my mom must have been praying for me. Her heart must have been hurting as she watched me in full self-destruction mode, knowing full well that what I saw and experienced at home, all due to Daddy's actions, was the biggest catalyst for my behavior and pain. I was so young, so naive, so broken, and so selfish. My heart breaks for my fifteen-year-old self.

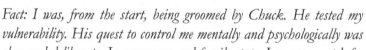

Fact: I was, from the start, being groomed by Chuck. He tested my vulnerability. His quest to control me mentally and psychologically was slow and deliberate. In my young and fragile state, I was no match for that old and seasoned predator.

Call to Action: I know life is busy and a lot of things are vying for our attention. Consider starting a daily ritual with your family to talk—really talk. No television. No cell phones. No distractions. Start small. Ten minutes. I promise, it'll be worth it!

Please see *Healing Waters: The Workbook* for more suggestions, exercises, and conversation starters. You'll also find information on the value of family time, both in the short term and its lifetime impact.

Angels watching over me

Shortly after we moved, I met a girl, Denise, who was a couple of years older than me. At only seventeen, she had her own apartment! I started hanging out at her house a lot! She seemed to be living in her own hell, though. She was addicted to heroin, had an infant daughter, and paid her bills by hooking and boosting clothes from department stores. Many times, I took care of her baby girl, Michelle, while she was out boosting or while she nodded off a high. If I was in a really good mood, I cleaned up her works and any blood she'd left in the bathroom after shooting up. When she wasn't too high or busy entertaining men for money, she'd show me how she could put two suits, a couple of dresses, and one or two coats in her specially made socks, underwear, and pants or dresses and look totally normal. A little heavier, maybe, but certainly not like she had hundreds or thousands of dollars' worth of clothing hidden underneath her outfits.

Soon after I started hanging out over there, her younger sister, Kim, who happened to be my age, moved in with her. She told me she was running away from her aunt and uncle's house because their son, her cousin, who was probably thirty years older than her, was sexually molesting her and her other sister regularly. Sadly, her aunt was not only aware of the molestation, but complicit in it. More than once, Kim told me, her aunt sent her or her sister upstairs to their molester as he called out to them. Even their tears and protests didn't save them. Their aunt told them to stop crying, insisting that he just wanted to talk to them and they needed to stop acting like babies! How does such evil exist? Kim also said this insane beast she called her aunt beat her all the time for no reason and her uncle never did anything about it.

Man, it seemed everybody I knew was hurting in some way. Anyway, I'm sure Kim thought moving in with her sister Denise had to be better than living with her aunt and uncle. Unfortunately, she'd soon find out that she was exchanging one hell for another.

Not long after Kim moved in, a new routine developed. While Denise was in bed, turning a trick, Kim would hide under the bed. Denise would make sure that he dropped his pants on the floor and while she went to work, Kim did, too. Kim "clipped the trick" by taking the money from his wallet and slipping the wallet back into his pants before they were finished.

Since Denise made sure he paid before they got in bed, he had no reason to check his wallet and he had usually long since left the apartment before he realized he'd been clipped. My job was to watch Denise's baby and keep her quiet in the living room while all of this was going on.

Once, for some reason, the trick checked his wallet as soon as he got downstairs. When he realized he'd been clipped, he started yelling and swearing from the street for Denise to give him his money back.

She was ducking so she couldn't be seen from the window, laughing. "Fuck him!" she said. "He ain't getting shit back! What's he gonna do, break in and take it?"

He went to his car and started honking his horn, still yelling. "Give me my money back, you bitch!" he screamed. He started picking up rocks and throwing them at the second-floor window.

I was holding Denise's baby, who had started to cry. "Stop it, Denise!" I said. "Just give the man his money back. You're scaring Michelle!"

"Fuck that!" she yelled. "I ain't giving him shit!"

Kim was close to tears. "Girl, damn! If you don't give it to him, I will. You want the police to show up at our door? You're so fuckin' stupid! Damn!" she said as she reached into her pocket, pulled out the money she'd taken and opened the window.

"Here!" she yelled at the man as she threw the money out the window. "Now stop all that screaming and get the fuck away from our house!"

"Fuck y'all, you nasty hos!" he said as he snatched up the bills and headed back to his car.

I continued rocking Michelle, trying to soothe her and get her to stop crying. "Whew!" I said. "We *all* dodged a bullet that time!" I was thinking about all the clothes, purses, and coats Denise had boosted that still had the tags on them. Plus, she had her heroin and her works on full display in her bathroom. We definitely did not need police in her apartment!

This hustle continued for months, until Denise told Kim she had to do more than just clip tricks to pay her way. She had to *turn* them, too—or get out! I begged her not to do it. I knew my house had its own craziness going on, but she and I had become close and I thought I could persuade my parents to let her share my room.

"Maybe you could get a regular job or go back to your aunt's house," I suggested after she declined my offer to live with me and my family.

"I don't have time to look for a job. Denise wants me to start giving her money *now*, and you know I'm not going back to that hellhole I came from!" she responded.

Sadly, Kim's own sister introduced her to a life of prostitution and all I could do was stand by and watch.

I continued to hang out over there, smoking weed or watching Michelle while they worked. One day as Kim and I sat getting high, talking about how she could get out of the life, Larry, the guy she worked for, showed up with his sister. Kim and Larry went into the bedroom to talk while his sister Cynthia and I sat in the living room, chatting. I guess Kim said or did something to piss him off because the next thing I heard was her crying and begging him to stop hitting her. Without thinking, I burst into the room and snatched at his arm to get him to quit beating her with the folded-over wire clothes hanger he had in his hand. He turned, raising his closed fist to punch me.

"Bitch! What's wrong with you?" he yelled at me. "This ain't got nothing to do with you! You need to stay outta this before you get hurt!"

I ducked just in time to avoid a smack to the face. "Leave her alone!" I said. "Whatever she did, she don't deserve you beating her like that!"

"Angel, stay out of it. I'm okay. I can handle myself," Kim interjected.

"Yeah, you need to listen to your friend before you git yo' ass beat!" he said.

Cynthia was at my side. "Girl, you don't know nothing about this! You really do need to stay out of it. That's their business. Let them handle their business before you get hurt." I looked at Kim and she gave me a sad glance before she looked away.

"Okay, then," I said. "I'm going home. Kim, call me later, okay?"

"Yeah, I will," she replied.

I left as quickly as I could. If the beating was going to start again, I couldn't be there to witness it and not do anything about it.

A couple of months later, Kim excitedly told me she was pregnant by her "employer," Larry. She said it was the best thing that could've happened to her because she wouldn't be able to work while she was pregnant. This was her way of getting out of the life for good.

I've gotta get out of here!

Even through all the insanity that was going on in every area of my life, I still went to school. School came easy for me. Doing homework, writing papers, and taking tests were all things I aced with very little effort. In fact, school bored me because it wasn't a challenge. If AP classes were available then, they were never offered to me. At the beginning of eleventh grade, when I turned sixteen, I realized I would have enough credits to graduate at the end of that year. I told my plan to the school counselor, Mr. Eikenberry, and he tried to talk me out of it, telling me I wasn't smart enough or ready to be out of school. He said I needed to find other classes I could take to get me through senior year. This low-expectations-having, shortsighted old man obviously knew nor cared anything about me. I ignored his "advice" and made sure I was enrolled in all the classes I needed to pass to walk at the end of the school year.

Daddy was mostly sober when he and the rest of my family came to my graduation. I could see, even then, that my daddy loved me, loved us, and as mad as I was at him for all the chaos and pain he brought into our lives, I loved him back. I could see his struggle to do better, be better, but those damn demons had settled into his being and refused to leave without a fight. Many of those same demons were chasing me and I, like my daddy, was ill-equipped to fight them off. I didn't realize it then, but for most of us, getting, being, and staying healthy are battles, and we need to be willing to call in all reinforcements if we want to win.

For me, this starts with a relationship with God that goes far below the surface. A relationship that never goes deeper than "Yeah, I believe" will get your spiritual teeth knocked out. Life isn't fair. It'll bust you in your face, kick you while you're down, and then stand over you, saying, "Get back up if you want to. I promise, I'll hit you again!" Getting up and staying up requires courage and a strategic plan.

> **Call To Action:** In our quest to "stay up" on our feet and move forward, I'd like to suggest that we all commit to honest accountability to ourselves and to others. That we work to give our best in every situation. That we take time to consider plans B, C, and D if our plan A fails. That we commit to showing up prepared. That we rebuke the lies told to us about our worth and abilities and create our own path rather than follow the crowd if that crowd is jumping off the cliff to destruction. I think it's worth repeating that I suggest we shamelessly check out therapy or coaching if we need help to interrupt unhealthy thoughts and behaviors.
>
> Check out *Healing Waters: The Workbook* for great exercises and resources that can help you create a plan to stay up and move forward.

Music and dancing don't make it a party

Graduating a year early gave me more time to work and party and I put more effort there than I had in school. I was back at Ward's full time and working part-time as a pharmacy technician, the job my mom helped me get at the hospital where she worked.

At only sixteen, I drank, smoked, and often partied all night. Many times, I arrived home in time to bathe and head right back out to work.

One night I was at a quarter party, dancing to Parliament Funkadelic's "Tear the Roof Off the Sucker" like I was trying to do just that.

Around 3:00 a.m., somebody called out, "Angel, your mom is here!"

I turned to see my beautiful mother coming down the stairs into the darkened basement, lit only by the upstairs light and the blue lights in the basement. "Hey Ma," I said as I kept dancing.

"Girl, I've been waiting for you at home! Come here!"

I turned to the boy I was dancing with. "My ma is here. I gotta go! See you!"

All my friends called out in near unison, "Bye, Ang! See you later!"

"Okay, see y'all!" I said almost gleefully as I scurried toward the stairs. My mom may have pulled me from the dance floor that night, but I was still dancing on the inside! I never felt one moment of embarrassment. I only felt joy! My Mommy came up for air from the craziness Daddy created long enough to know that I needed her! My Ma cared enough to come and find me in the middle of the night. She didn't care one bit about how it might look when she came to take me home.

When we got in the car, she put her hand on mine and said, "Honey, you're better than this. You've gotta think about your choices. Do you wanna talk?"

"Nah, I'm okay," I responded as I looked out the window, still buzzed from the weed we'd smoked earlier. "I'm sleepy. I have to be at work at seven."

She looked at me sadly, squeezed my hand, and said, "Okay. You know I'm here if you wanna talk."

As happy as I was that my mom loved me enough to come and get me in the middle of the night, I still didn't open up to her to tell her about my anger, pain, and fear. If only we had actively sought out something or someone to interrupt this path of destruction I was heading down full speed, I might have avoided stumbling through years of devastating pain and heartache.

Water finds its level

In the meantime, Daddy decided he wanted to try sobriety again and yet again joined AA. He met another woman there who was far less interested in sobriety than he was. The AA tenets didn't stick, but the chick did. This "woman" was only a few years older than me. She was also a notorious prostitute who worked the local factories, turning tricks. Many people, including relatives, told me they had constantly warned Daddy that this chick was a trick he should stay away from.

He ignored their advice. While still living in our home, he began yet another torrid affair with her that included tons of alcohol, disrespect, and abuse. She called the house asking for my dad on a daily basis. She was, without reservation, nasty to my mom. I regularly took the phone from my mom if she got to it first and cussed this disrespectful common streetwalker out every chance I got. I begged her to come over so I could beat her ass. She never had the nerve to show up and I set my sights on getting out of there.

My daddy chose this trick over my virtuous, amazing, loving, ride-or-die, hold-it-down-without-complaint, beautiful-inside-and-out mother and his three amazing, love-you need-you want-you, well-raised—at least until he came home—children!

A year or two later, after I'd left for college, my father told me this prostitute was pregnant and he didn't want that child to suffer the same fate that the three of us had. Given the woman's reputation, what made him believe the baby was his, I didn't understand. Still, he said he saw this child as an opportunity to make amends and "get it right." He said he was going to stay sober this time, marry the prostitute, and work on his relationship with us three children as well. Sadly, he unceremoniously left our mother for good this time and they got divorced. I say sadly only because it dashed my mother's hopes that things would turn around and the two of them could live the dream she'd been nurturing for over a decade.

Most of Daddy's family and friends believed marrying that woman was the worst mistake he could have made. All too late, he came to believe it, too. She was a lying, two-faced, adulterous shrew and I began to refer to her as the "evil step-monster."

Curiously, both this woman and Thing were white. Many years later, I asked my daddy why he'd chosen white women over our beautiful black mother. I was expecting him to say something I could understand and respect, like "I just fell in love, honey, and love has no color." Instead he said he had never loved either of them, but saw his choice as a way to get back at white people for all the pain and trauma they'd caused him throughout his life.

"Why didn't you consider that loving your black wife and children, being a positive force in our lives and creating a strong, intact, healthy family unit would be the best revenge possible?" I asked.

"I don't know, honey. I was hurting and blinded by rage. Again, I'm sorry I hurt you."

Tears rolled down my cheeks and the lump in my throat kept me from responding as I let myself be pulled into his embrace.

"I really wish I could do things over," he whispered as he held me.

"Yeah, me, too," I thought.

Chapter 15

Same Soup, Different Bowl

Running without a plan is like running in place—all you get is tired

I knew I wanted to go away to college and my mom, as always, came through for me again. We spent countless hours in the library researching grants and scholarships, talking about what course of study I might be interested in, and considering what schools to apply to. My goal was to enroll *somewhere* in the spring semester after sitting out the fall semester.

As wild and crazy as my life was, I still attended church periodically and always stayed close to a few of the people who went there. One girl, Sheila, who is to this day a dear friend, had left for Illinois State University the semester before and we began talking about me joining her there. She even offered for us to be roommates. I'd always dreamed of getting farther away; Normal was *way* too close to Rockford and I might be tempted to come back! Still, after many conversations with her and my mom, I agreed to apply. Of course I was accepted and within a few months I was embarking on a new adventure.

My entire family, including my daddy, drove me down to Illinois State. It was a celebration! Even though my mom was a very accomplished and respected registered nurse at her hospital—as I mentioned, she started the outpatient surgery unit, wrote the manual, determined the staff requirements, helped with the unit's design, and hired and managed the entire staff, all while under insane stress and chaos at home—I was still the first one in our entire family, including all of my parents' siblings and their children, to attend a four-year college.

While I was off starting a new (but not necessarily better) life, things at home were business as usual, but on steroids. My brother later told me that Daddy was still an abusive tyrant, arguing, yelling, and swearing at them regularly. The prostitute was still in the picture and he would go to see her (and other women), then come back home like Mom was just the maid or something.

The fights and threats continued. My sister left for college and my brother was left alone with all of this madness going on between my parents. Daddy was dishing out abuse and Mom was taking it. I never once remember my mother saying anything negative about my dad! The most she would say was, "He's your dad. I love him. You guys need to work your relationship out with him and let his actions and behavior determine how you feel about him, but try to understand and forgive him, if you can."

I think my mom is amazing in her ability to forgive and try to move on, but she also taught me how to accept way too much disrespect, how to put myself last and love some man more than I love myself.

School Dayz

Sheila was a great roommate! She took me under her wing as best she could, listening to my woes and quietly suggesting healthy options. She introduced me to people who had their heads on straight and were studious, yet cool. While I appreciated her friendship and concern, I was still wild and rebellious. I hung with her crew, but I quickly found the party crowd on campus and spent just as much time with them. Just like at home, school came easily for me. I really did love to learn and I loved being in class. It just seemed that I loved smoking weed almost as much and I had too many people around me who loved it more than I did.

Fortunately, Chuck had grown tired of me after several months of abuse and moved on, I'm sure, to another young, vulnerable girl. I was still seeing LT, though. Even at seven foot one, he wasn't a phenom on the basketball court, so he settled for a full basketball scholarship to a small school in Kenosha, Wisconsin.

Almost immediately after I arrived at ISU, he began sending me money to take the train to see him, which I did at least twice a month. Once I was there, the party continued. He lived off campus in an apartment building full of other members of the basketball team and their girlfriends. Every night was a party! White boys seemed to have the best weed and they were happy to supply the star athletes with as much as they could handle in exchange for being able to hang out with them.

In the beginning, I left ISU on Friday evening and returned Sunday so I could be in class on Monday. Eventually, though, I'd be gone for a week or more at a time. Sheila told me years later that she was amazed at how I could come in a day or two before a test or when a major paper was due, stay up all night cramming, then get an A on the assignment! It saddens me to think what I could have been or done had I consistently gone to class and focused.

A few teachers saw my potential and tried to get me to see it, too. Once, a beautiful soul that lived inside a young black writing professor asked me to stand and read Dr. King's "I Have a Dream" speech. I could see in his eyes that he knew I had a gift for writing and oratory delivery. I'd always gotten A's or B's on every paper I'd turned in and he regularly praised my work. That day, though, I was fatigued and probably hung over from a long weekend of partying. I gave a lackluster delivery of the speech and took my seat. The look of hurt and disappointment in his eyes shamed me, but sadly, not enough to stop this train of destruction I seemed determined to ride.

When the semester ended, I didn't want to go home, so I enrolled in both pre-session and summer school, getting good grades and racking up school credits with an eye already toward graduation.

Regret

In July, the next stop on my train ride of destruction was one missed period and then another. No way! I cannot be pregnant! I thought. This is the last thing I need! I was only seventeen and finishing my first year of college. I called LT to deliver the news. He asked me what I wanted to do, but only after suggesting that this wasn't a good time for either of us. I agreed and told him I needed to be home, near my mom, when I had the procedure.

I scheduled it for a Friday in Rockford and he promised to be in Rockford to take me and pick me up. I came home on Wednesday and moped around the house, hoping my mom would ask me what was wrong so I could reveal my secret and she could save me from what I knew was a horrible mistake. She was loving and glad I was home, but she was too preoccupied with Daddy's nonsense to notice that something was really wrong.

On Friday, LT picked me up and drove me to make one of the saddest mistakes of my life—and there have been many. He dropped me off and went to play basketball, leaving me to go through this experience all alone. The attending nurse was kind. She held my hand and wiped my tears during the painful procedure. LT picked me up and we rode in silence back to my mom's house. I spent most of the weekend on the couch, not saying much to anyone. I took my secret with me back to school on Sunday. It took years for me to tell my mom what had happened and when I did, we cried together while she held me and apologized for not being more present for me. I never blamed my mom for the choice I made and I told her that. I know she feels sad about many of the things I experienced, but more importantly, I know she loves me and did her absolute best every single day to be the best mom she could. She did, and continues to do, a fabulous job.

Classic codependent behavior

In August of that year, LT tore his Achilles tendon and his mom— yep, the one who never liked me—asked me to take a semester off from school to move to Kenosha, Wisconsin, and care for her "baby."

My self-esteem was firmly in the toilet, so I said, "Of course I'll go, Mary! Thank you for thinking I could do this!" Crazy, right? Lord, did I need help! Mary recognized my love, strength, and ability to do what she asked. She also knew I was weak enough for her to exploit all of that and manipulate me, which she did masterfully. I wasn't going to turn eighteen until that September, so my godsend of a mom stepped in.

"Absolutely not!" she said. "I know you think you're grown, but you are still *my* baby and *my* responsibility. You're gonna enroll in the fall semester and stay focused on you!"

Thank you, Mommy, for loving me!

I wish she hadn't, but she went on to say, "When you turn eighteen, you are legally grown and I can't stop you, but I wish you would stay in school."

So, I enrolled in classes for that fall semester and let the "devious duo" work on me for months to convince me that LT "needed me" and how much it would mean to both of them if I would "just go for a few months to help him out." Looking back, this makes absolutely no sense; he tore his Achilles tendon in August. By January, he should have been well on his way to being healed. I know it sounds crazy, but I finished the fall semester, then, wiping the tears from my mom's face, got in the car with LT and moved to Kenosha to support his "healing."

Once there, I kept up my "program" and immediately found a full-time job at a bank.

Since the day my mom's friend, Joyce, told me she'd made $36,000 in commission from the sale of one farm, I'd been fascinated with real estate, so I enrolled in a class to get my license. I thought that was so cool because in Wisconsin, you only had to be eighteen to get a license, while you had to wait until twenty-one to be licensed in Illinois.

God blessed me (and you) with superpowers. One of mine was to be able to trip through life while still falling forward. I am *finally* absolutely certain that there is greatness in each of us, that we are all "fearfully and wonderfully made." We are resilient, creative, and beautiful. We each have something special to give to the world. I finally get it that my responsibility is to listen to my inner voice so I can nurture my innate gifts. I hope that if you aren't already, you'll be inspired to do the same. By now you know I'm a big advocate for creating a team to support your health and success, so you won't be surprised to hear me suggest here that if you're feeling challenged in identifying your voice, your gifts, or your calling, please don't hesitate to seek out a good coach.

While I continued to pursue my goals, I also continued to indulge in unhealthy behaviors. Instead of encouraging me in my real estate studies, LT always had an apartment full of teammates, friends, and hangers-on, all there to smoke, drink, and party into the night. Too often, I was right there with them while somehow finding the time and energy to work, go to class, and study. I also cooked and cleaned while LT "recovered from his injury" and went to a class or two during the week.

His mom bought him a car and sent him money every month, but I took the bus to work every morning and paid half the bills. Any money I had left over, I saved in anticipation of returning to school in the fall.

Does any of this sound familiar? I didn't make the connection at the time, but I was mirroring my parents relationship to a T!

I met a really cool sister, Connie Benitez (call me, girl!) whom I smoked weed with, but who, more importantly, became my only friend in Kenosha. We shared our hopes and dreams, encouraged each other, spoke life into each other, and reminded each other that we were better than our circumstances suggested.

The night before I was scheduled to take my real estate exam, LT decided to throw a blowout of a party. He had more people over than usual, asked me to cook (I refused. Yay, Angel!) and blasted the music all evening and late into the night. I locked myself in our bedroom and shut out the noise as best I could to focus on studying. After only a few hours of rest, I was up and ready to go. I stepped over beer bottles, empty plates, and full ashtrays and left LT sleeping while I ran to catch the bus to take my exam. I wish I could say that I passed, but I failed by only two points. I think the fact that I came so close to passing made the disappointment even greater. In retrospect, I now know that my failing was another blessing. Had I passed, I'm sure I would have stayed in Wisconsin to work. I may never have finished college and I most certainly would have entered an abusive marriage and gotten an abusive mother-in-law to go with it.

LT didn't console me, but offered me a toke off the joint he was smoking when I walked in and shared the news. Then he asked me what I was planning to cook for dinner! It was like he was happy that I'd failed.

I decided right then that I was going home. I left in August, but hadn't reenrolled in school. When I got back to my mom's house, I bought a car with some of the money I was able to save and found a job. I decided I wanted to get as far away from LT as possible, so I persuaded my mom to ask her friend who lived in Northern California if I could live with her long enough to gain residency and enroll at Berkeley. She never responded and I feel bad that I may have injured their relationship by making such a huge request. I reenrolled at ISU and set my sights on returning there for the spring semester.

Not at all surprisingly, LT's mom accused me of "taking a vacation instead of taking care of her son and living off her so I could take my money to buy a car." That woman really was a selfish, abusive, delusional ingrate and I'm so thankful I never had to call her mother-in-law.

Not more than a month after I returned back to Rockford from Kenosha, as I drove through an intersection about two blocks from our house, I was T-boned by car driven by a teenaged white boy. The speed limit on these neighborhood side streets was only 20 mph, but this guy was zooming along at more than 40mph! He slammed into my driver's side just behind where I was sitting, sending my car spinning round and round until it finally landed nearly half a block away, stopped only by a tree. Miraculously, although my new-to-me car was totaled, I only suffered a few bruises and a sprained wrist! The guy who hit me was a little shaken, but he wasn't hurt at all. His car, bigger and heavier than mine, was only dented.

When the police arrived, they gave me the ticket, saying that I'd failed to yield the right-of-way in an unmarked intersection! Even though he was going more twice the speed limit, he didn't even get a warning.

When we went to court a month later, I showed up alone because my mom was working and my dad just wasn't that guy. The judge agreed with the police officer who came to the scene and let my ticket stand while giving the speeder a "good luck in your future; glad you weren't hurt" speech.

To say I was already exhausted at only eighteen, from a lifetime of gut punches, was a major understatement. I dug deep, though, and prepared to head back to Illinois State on the bus, the same way I'd gone the first time.

When I got back to school, LT and I continued to see each other, but not nearly as frequently. I was growing tired of his needy, whiny, selfish behavior. (Apple trees bear apples!) His grades weren't good and when he was offered a spot on a basketball team in France, he left school behind and took it.

While he was overseas, we continued to talk on the phone and write. In February, three months before I was scheduled to graduate— on time, with my class, even though I'd sat out for a year—he begged me to leave school right away and join him.

"I'm so lonely here without you. Please come, baby! I miss you and I love you! Plus, it's getting hard to stay faithful," he said.

Really? I thought. You weren't faithful when I lived ten blocks from you!

But I said, "You know I'm graduating in three months. That's no time. I'll come after I walk."

"No, I need you to come now! We can't build our dreams at the same time. You come and support me in mine and once my career is solid, you can go back to school and get your degree. I'll support you then if you support me now," he pleaded.

"You're joking, right? You wouldn't ask me to quit when I'm this close, would you?" I asked, incredulous.

The rest of the conversation is unimportant. The result was that was the last nail in the coffin of our already dying relationship. I went on to enter other abusive relationships, but this selfish disrespect was just too blatant for even me to bear.

Call to Action: Self-love is paramount to a healthy mindset and life. Learn to pay attention to how you allow people to treat and speak to you.

Please see *Healing Waters: The Workbook* for exercises on assessing your "self-love tank" and learning to truly fall in love with yourself.

Chapter 16

New Beginnings: Chicago, Here I Come!

Everywhere you go, there you are

I graduated, moved back to Rockford, immediately enrolled in real estate school, passed the test with ease and started working as a realtor. I also took a job as head of the youth division of the local chapter of Operation Push. This took me to Chicago often and by February, less than a year out of college, I'd packed my bags and moved in with an older woman, Dee, whom I met at Operation Push's Chicago office. Dee and I hit it off right away and she claimed she wanted to take me under her wing and help me get settled in the city.

At first, everything was great. I volunteered a lot at Push and got a job as a travel agent. Dee lived on the fortieth floor of a beautiful building on Chicago's Gold Coast. Her only child was away at school in Hawaii, so I had an en suite to myself with floor-to-ceiling windows overlooking the lake.

It was a heady time. Operation Push welcomed many celebrities, both locally and nationally known, and I got to meet and spend time with many of them. I got to know the Jackson family, spending time with them at their lovely home and I found them all to be gracious and down to earth. I worked on Harold Washington's first mayoral campaign and was fortunate to spend hours at his home, sharing good meals and listening much more than talking, to his sage advice and position on the needs and concerns of the people of Chicago.

One day, as I left the building on my way to enjoy the neighborhood, I saw Chuck! Yeah, *that* Chuck!

"Angel? Is that you? What are you doing here?"

"Hey, Chuck. Yeah, it's me. I live here now."

"Oh wow! You live *here*?" he asked, amazed.

"Yeah, staying with a friend. What's up?" I said, hoping he'd keep it movin'.

One thing led to another and somehow I agreed to go to his house on the west side for drinks.

WTF, right? I know, I really needed therapy! Anyway, we walked to his car and on the ride to his house, I could see that nothing had changed.

"Damn, you look *good*!"

"Yeah, thanks," I said, wondering what I'd gotten myself into.

"Oh, I've thought about you a lot over the years and I wanted to apologize for the way I treated you. You didn't deserve that. I was just so attracted to you. You were, you are, just so beautiful. I don't know what I was thinking."

Yeah, right. Your nasty ass knew exactly what you were thinking *and* doing, I thought, but I said, "Yeah, you really hurt me."

"Well, I hope you can forgive me."

When I didn't respond, we rode the rest of the way, looking out the window and making small talk. On the way, we stopped at his mom's to pick up his son. We got to his house, had a few drinks, and before I knew it, it was almost 10:00 p.m.

As he headed into the kitchen with our glasses, Chuck said, "I'm tired. Plus, I don't wanna take the baby out. Why don't you just stay here and I'll take you home in the morning? You can sleep in my bed and I'll sleep on the couch. If you hear something in the middle of the night, it's just me checking on my son."

"Okay, that's cool," I responded.

I laid down on top of the covers in the shorts and T-shirt I had arrived in. I lay there for a long time, listening to the sounds of the night and to his baby sleeping soundly. Eventually, I drifted off.

I was startled awake by Chuck laying on top of me, my hands being held together above my head by one of his, while his other hand was working to unbutton my shorts and pull them down.

"What are you doing? Stop!" I screamed.

It was like he was in a trance. He didn't say one word. He just kept pulling at my shorts as he tightened his grip on my wrists above my head.

He's done this before, I thought. He knew exactly how to restrain me. This thought scared me and fueled me at the same time. I couldn't let him rape me again!

"Please stop! Please!" I begged as I twisted and turned, trying to get him to roll off of me.

Finally, he spoke. "Shut the fuck up before you wake up my son!" he hissed.

Oh, that's my out—his son! I yelled even louder. "Stop! Let go of me! Leave me alone!"

The only thing that makes sense is that my guardian angels were watching over me because he just . . . stopped. He looked down at me, and I stopped struggling and met his gaze.

After what felt like forever, he released his grip on my wrists, rolled off of me, and said, "Get the fuck out."

I got up, buttoned my shorts, and made my way out the door and into the night. At about two in the morning, I walked the streets of the west side, scared to death, but not as scared as I'd been with Chuck, and found my way to the 'L.' Once I got on the train, I released a torrent of tears, both from the gratitude of not being raped again or worse and from knowing that through it all, I still had guardian angels watching over and protecting me. "Lord, please just help me to hear Your voice," I prayed.

I didn't understand then that prayer wasn't enough. Study and listening are also required. Now, for those of you who might be saying, "Oh, here we go with the religious stuff," hang in here with me. That still, small voice exists in each of us. You might be more comfortable calling it intuition or a "knowing," but it's there.

Fortunately for us, God isn't hung up on religion. The important thing is that we commit to a relationship with Him. That we carve out time in our daily routine to be quiet and listen and, once we've heard, that we trust His voice and act accordingly. If you'll give reading the Bible a chance, you'll be not only pleasantly surprised, but amazed at the wisdom found in the scriptures. There is nothing you can face that doesn't come with a clear answer in the Bible. Please don't take my word for it; check it out for yourself. I promise you won't be disappointed.

"Friend" is a verb

"Smiling faces sometimes pretend to be your friend."
Undisputed Truth

Smiling Faces

I also met quite a few men with money who contributed to political campaigns and to Operation Push. Before long, Dee was telling me that having me in her home was "expensive" and I "needed to accept the offers from these guys who liked me."

"You've gotta be kidding!" I responded. "I'm not sleeping with those old-ass men!"

"Really? Girl, sometimes you've gotta do what you have to to get what you want. You think it's cheap living here? There are worse ways to get paid. You need to figure something out. I'm going back up to Push for a couple of hours. You wanna come?" she asked as she headed back toward her room to change her clothes.

"Nah, I'm gonna call my mom and clean the bathrooms. I'll see you when you get back." I needed time to process what she'd just said. Her home was beautiful. I loved living on the Gold Coast, but I definitely wasn't going to start prostituting myself to stay there. I convinced myself she didn't really mean it and she wouldn't really expect me to sell my body to pay the rent. I let it go and she seemed to as well.

A couple of weeks later, one fat, unattractive guy at least thirty-five years older than me again offered me five hundred dollars to let him perform oral sex on me. I saw him often at Operation Push. He was also a friend of Dee's, so he stopped by the house periodically. Again, I declined, but this time I told Dee about it. I knew how she thought, but I wasn't expecting her response to be at ten.

She cursed me out for about fifteen minutes. Then she dropped the bomb: if I didn't start contributing significantly to the household, I had to move and I had thirty days "to get her some money!" Even though I talked to my mom every day, it took me a week of crying myself to sleep every night, trying to figure out what to do, to tell her what was going on. She suggested I either come home or call her sister to see if I could stay with her and her husband until I could find my own apartment. The timing was good because my cousins were away at school and the marines, so they had the space. I chose the latter and called my aunt that evening.

As I mentioned before, Mom always made sure she kept us connected to our aunts, uncles, and cousins. Before Daddy came home, Mommy loaded us three kids into the car at least once a month during the summer and we made our way east to Chicago's south side to spend time with Aunt Elois, her husband, and their two children. We remained close and when I moved to Chicago, I visited them regularly.

I think my mom had already called her sister to tell her to expect my call, because I'd barely gotten my request out before she responded with an immediate and enthusiastic yes! Rather than wait until the end of the month, I thanked Dee for her hospitality and headed south.

As I packed to leave, I noticed an expensive gold chain with a beautiful pendant, the only decent piece of jewelry I owned at the time, was missing. I asked Dee about it and she claimed she didn't know what I was talking about. She and I were the only two living in the house, so of course she took it. I guess she decided I owed her "back rent." I didn't argue; I was just glad to be moving out of her house before she could try to pimp me out again. I'm also thankful for another lesson she made sure I learned. She taught me to closely watch the behavior of a person and how they live their lives *before* I begin any type of relationship with them. If I see them disrespecting anyone, even a waiter in a restaurant, I take note. They are telling me who they are. Now I don't delude myself into thinking I'm somehow special and I won't get a turn at the receiving end of their disrespect. I no longer tell myself they deserve a second chance. As the wise sage, Maya Angelou, who now sits with our ancestors, said, "When people show you who they are, believe them the first time."

Welcome arms

"As one whom his mother comforts, so will I comfort you" (Isaiah 66:23).

My aunt and uncle's home was modest compared to Dee's, but it was warm and full of love, laughter, and great food. I still went home almost every weekend; I just loved being around my mom and I felt I needed to check on her as she was still grieving the end of her marriage. It was during this time that Aunt Elois and I became really close. We shopped together, cooked and ate together, went to church together, and just hung out as much as we could. I thank God for that time with her. She poured into me and laid a solid foundation that would serve to catch me when I fell a few short years later.

Soon after I moved south, I left the travel agency and started a job as a Drug and Pregnancy Prevention Coordinator at Community Linkages. I loved that job! My manager, Diane Cotton, was a really cool sister with a beautiful spirit. She encouraged me in my work, gave me the space to grow, and always had a listening ear and sound advice. Together we wrote curriculum, then delivered the programs to the children in elementary and middle schools. I loved those children and they loved me. Some of the things they'd seen and experienced at their tender ages were heartbreaking, but they were still so full of love, life, and hope. This question has been asked for years, but why do the jobs that can make the most difference so often pay the least? Because of my family's generosity, though, I didn't have to pay much in the way of rent, so I was able to buy a car and save a few dollars in anticipation of buying or renting my own place.

I have another aunt, Aunt Candy, whom I also absolutely adore. I was blessed to spend almost as much time with her and her family as I did at home with Aunt Elois and Uncle Milton. Both of my aunts poured into me in their own ways and my Aunt Candy, a former executive at Xerox, eventually prepared me to interview for the sales job I applied for and got at Xerox when I realized I would never be able to move out on my own if I stayed at Community Linkages.

My life was no different from yours or anybody else's in that there was some really good stuff to offset the bad. As I continued to make a life for myself in Chicago, I also joined a women's organization, the National Hookup of Black Women, and met its founder, Dr. Arnita Young Boswell. She's the sister of the famed Whitney Young, a former executive director of the National Urban League and was an absolute powerhouse in her own right. She was the founder of this organization and others, active in civil and women's rights, an advocate for children, a writer, a speaker, and an educator.

And she was my friend. She took me into her home and her life, and I came to adopt her as my godmother. We spent countless hours together, eating out or preparing meals at her home. We often went to one of the many functions she was always invited to or attended meetings for one of the organizations she had started. Often we'd just sit in her living room, talking. Her daughter Bonnie and her family embraced me as well. Dr. B poured into me in so many ways. She encouraged and challenged me. She talked with me and probed me to think about my life and my choices. She was yet another gift from God and I'm grateful for the years we had together as friends. She, too, now sits with our ancestors and although I really miss her presence in my life, the love and wisdom she gave me fuels and sustains me.

But still, I kept running into emotional brick walls.

Call to Action: Practice adding "pauses" to your day to breathe and reflect. This will help you recognize those who bring positive energy to your world and those who don't. People and experiences are always "talking" to us; we just have to take the time to listen. Of course, you want to embrace those who have a positive influence!

Please see *Healing Waters: The Workbook* for exercises on mindfulness and guided meditations to help you "see" within you and around you.

Chapter 17

Still Young, Still Dumb

◆━━━━━━━◆━━━━━━━◆

"At some point, you have to stop crossing oceans for people who wouldn't even jump puddles for you." —*Anonymous*

I was fully aware that something wasn't right with me, that I'd been on the receiving end of too much abuse, and I actively looked for ways to be and feel better. I started going to therapy, went to church a lot and lived in my Bible, looking for answers and relief. More often than not, I had my Bible with me so I could study it when I had a moment.

One day as I was getting my car washed, I met a new demon, who used the name Tony to fit in with us humans.

"Hey, beautiful! Why isn't your man washing your car for you? If I was your man, I'd keep your car clean all the time!" this gremlin disguised as a normal human being said to me with a big smile.

"I don't have a man," I said, returning the smile with eagerness like the lonely, insecure, attention-starved girl I was. "Plus, I'm perfectly capable of keeping my own car clean," I said, feigning confidence.

"What?! *You* don't have a man? As fine as you are? Nobody's snatched you up yet?" this wannabe hustler asked me as he moved in for the kill.

At the time, though, all my thirsty behind saw was an older man giving me the attention I craved in an attempt to fill the void left by what I felt was the loss of my father's love.

That day was the beginning of a whirlwind experience that was too twisted to be called a romance. Tony lied from the minute we met, telling me how much money he had from the success of his medical transportation business and the rental property he owned.

"Let's drive your car," he'd say. "My Benz is still in the shop."

"Still? What's wrong with it? It's been almost a month. I don't mind always driving, but you must want your car back," I'd respond when, yet again, he called me to pick him up in my Volkswagen.

"Yeah, I do, but they say I need a new engine. Matter of fact, you mind if I drop you off at work and keep your car to collect my rents?"

As the famed poet and songstress, my girl Jilly from Philly, would say, my "being vulnerable made the obvious invisible." The obvious was that Tony was a raging dope fiend, a liar, a cheat, a sadist, a con artist, an insecure user, and an abuser.

Once when I was still a Bible-toting innocent, we stopped—in my car because, as it turned out, he didn't have one—at his friend's house for him to pick up some drugs. He took my keys and left me in that car, my car, by myself late at night in a less-than-desirable area for well over an hour. He obviously couldn't have cared less about my safety or my well-being.

While he was inside, I felt in every cell of my being that I should run! I opened my Bible and prayed for guidance. I turned to the scripture that tells us to forgive seven times seventy and to forgive if we want to be forgiven (Matthew 18).

I thought back to all the times I'd done things I wasn't proud of, all the times I'd done things that I'd begged God to forgive me for: the abortion, the copious drug consumption, the fights with my father, the sexual abuse (Oh, right—that wasn't my fault, was it? Why, then, did I believe it was?) and I felt like that was God telling me to forgive this man, too.

What I understand now is that the enemy knows the Bible better than we do and will use it to trip us up; rob us of peace; convince us of lies about ourselves, our experiences, and the world; and, if possible, kill us! What I know now is that just reading the Bible isn't enough. It tells us to watch as well as pray, to ask God for wisdom and discernment. The Bible clearly tells us what the enemy comes for: to steal, kill, and destroy. Knowing this and applying this knowledge has to be a part of every equation, every experience, every choice. When something doesn't feel right, doesn't look right, doesn't line up with

God's word or that inner knowing and common sense, follow your gut and run!

One of the biggest things I missed was that I had my mom, my Aunt Candy, my Aunt Elois and Dr. B, all who loved me very much and wanted the best for me. Any of the four of them, if I'd had sense enough to share my experiences and thoughts with them, would have advised me to leave this demon seed alone. Knowing what I know now, I would advise every young person to take advantage of the wisdom and experience of the adults in their life. They can help sort things out so that healthier decisions can be made.

At the time, though, I possessed only tattered self-esteem and I lacked the wisdom and common sense to know or apply any of this or seek the counsel of those who loved me. Instead, I believed that if I turned to this passage about forgiveness, it must be God's will. Even though it didn't feel right, not only did I forgive Tony, but I leaned in even more. He drove my car, spent my money, and knocked my twenty-two-year-old head like that was his job.

One night, we walked into his darkened house, laughing and talking, and he was kissing me (yuck!). After we'd been in the house for several minutes, he finally reached for the light switch on the wall, flipped it on, and there sat his baby's momma! She was sitting in a chair in the dark, watching and listening to everything we said and did! She scared me to death! She reminded me of Glenn Close in *Fatal Attraction!* After a forty-five-second shocked face-off, this crazed woman jumped out of her chair and, screaming, charged toward us. She attacked this trifling monster for cheating on *her*. I just stood there for a minute, trying to understand what was happening. Both of them yelling at me, telling me to leave, finally snapped me out of the daze I was in. I snatched my keys from where he'd dropped them, ran out the door, hopped into my car, and sped away.

What a blessing it would have been if that were the end of this story. But, nooo . . . he called me over and over and eventually wooed me back. Even with all the flashing lights, sirens, bells, and whistles warning me otherwise, I was still playing the role of my mother while he nailed my daddy's role like he'd written it.

Somehow, only a few short months after I met this Lucifer, I found myself standing before the then well-known Father Clements at Holy Angels Catholic Church. There, in front of Tony's family and mine, my daddy included, I vowed to spend my life with him for better or for worse. That was one vow I desperately sought to break less than two years later because there was no "better" and the bad only continued to get worse.

Right before the wedding, God spoke to me from more than one "burning bush," but I was completely hoodwinked. I just thought the light in my eyes was love, not the oncoming train bearing down to crush me that it really was. The first major sign came from LT. The night before I was to marry, my sister was spending the night with me to help me get ready and just be the dear friend that she was and still is. The phone rang. It was LT telling me he was in town, visiting from France and staying at a hotel near the airport.

"Please come out and spend some time with me. I've really missed you and I want us to try to work it out," he pleaded.

"Sure, I'll come out for a minute, but I can't stay long. I've got a busy day tomorrow." I didn't even tell him I was getting married in less than twenty-four hours.

When I showed up an hour later with my sister in tow, he was shocked and disappointed. "Hey, Deb, what are you doing here?" he asked.

"Hey, LT! Good to see you, too!" she joked.

"Yeah, of course, good seeing you, but I'm just surprised. I really wanted to spend some time with Ang alone."

"Oh, yeah, I'm not staying here in the room with you guys. I'll be in the lobby. I just wanted to say hi," she responded as she gave me a quick hug and turned to leave.

"I'll see you in a few minutes, Sis," I said as I closed the door.

"Why'd you bring her?" he whined as soon as I'd turned back to him. "I wanted you to spend the night. I want us to be together. I missed you. I want you to come back to France with me."

"I really appreciate all that, LT, but I can't. What we had is over. Too much time has passed. I've moved on. Plus, I feel like you never really respected me or appreciated me. I don't believe you've changed."

"I have changed. I love you. I'm making good money now and I can take care of you. You won't have to work. You can just enjoy Europe and even go back to school and get another degree, if you want!"

"No," I replied, "I just really wanted to see you again, but I can't go back with you. I hope we'll always be friends and you know I wish you the best."

I left the room with both of us in tears. As difficult as most of our relationship had been, he was my first love. The next day, as my mom, sister, and I were standing in a dressing room at Holy Angels Church, my mom gently held my face in her hands and said, "Honey, you don't have to do this. It's not too late to just walk away. We can get in the car and leave right now. You'll be fine. We'll make sure of it."

Now, if this wasn't a burning bush, I don't know what is! Instead of heeding the warning and listening to my mom, one of the wisest and most intuitive women I've ever known, I said, "No, Ma, I'm okay. I want to do this. I love him and he loves me." Lord, how young, wounded, and dumb I was!

"Okaaay, but you need to remember that you can always walk away and come home if you need to. There is no shame in leaving if you feel it's not right. I am, we are, just a phone call away."

Do you ever wish you didn't have so much free will? I know I do! I wish my mom had strong-armed me and said, "Girl, get your naive, therapy-needing butt in this car! That old man is straight from hell and I will not let him have you!"

She didn't say that, and I made yet another huge mistake that would wound my soul and take me years to escape and recover from.

"You remind me of a haunted house I once was in."
—Lee Oskar

This twisted loser hardly worked the whole time I knew him. He was always working on "the next big thing." He held temporary and part-time jobs, but nothing substantial.

Leading up to our doomed-from-the-start marriage, he thought it'd be a great idea if "we" bought a condo in Hyde Park. I readily agreed. I applied and qualified for the purchase of a beautiful two-bedroom, two-bath condo with a parking space steps from Lake Michigan. Shortly after we moved in, I got the sales job at Xerox that my Aunt Candy had coached me for.

In the winter, I would go downstairs to clean off and start the car to warm it up. More often than not, when I came back into the house, I'd catch that demon running from the second bathroom like he'd just hidden something and I'd smell an odd, sweet odor in the house. It turns out he'd been smoking crack cocaine the whole time we were together and it had started long before I came on the scene.

My job, especially when I first started, took me to Virginia for weeks at a time for training. I later learned from one of the many women he was seeing that during my times away, she was there often, having sex all over my house. She told me she felt the love and peace there the first time she visited. She said she knew it was wrong, but she "loved" him and wanted to be with him, so she enjoyed my home, had sex with my husband, and slept in my bed while I was away. She told me it "wasn't personal" and they'd been together the day before we got married. She also shared with me that they smoked crack together and she was surprised I didn't know.

He also introduced me to another woman, September. She had been in a horrible car accident years earlier and lost both of her legs. She visited our home and we visited hers. She had prosthetic limbs that she deftly used, but would remove them when I or we visited her at her home. We spent tons of time together, sharing meals, laughs, and weed. It turns out that during this entire time, she and my twisted, evil "husband" were engaged in a hot and heavy affair. During a conversation she and I had after I finally left him, she told me they'd had sex in her house, our house, my car, and anywhere else they thought might be fun. More than once, she said, I almost caught them in the act. Their affair started before we were married and continued after I left his nasty ass.

After we divorced, I asked him about her. He said she'd meant nothing to him, that he thought it was "interesting to have sex with a woman with no legs." That comment clearly shows how soulless he was. Getting away from him with my life, health, and sanity has been just one of God's many blessings in my life.

Before I learned of all of his infidelities, though, I tried hard to make things work. I did everything I thought a good wife was supposed to do. I worked, paid the bills, cooked, and cleaned, all while supporting his "dreams," which were just smoke and mirrors to hide his real goal: living off of me, getting high, and having affairs.

They smilin' in your face
All the time they want to take your place
The backstabbers

The O'Jays, Backstabbers

Not long after we were married, my sister-aunt Lynn, whom I was now in regular contact with and who had been in and out of prison for several years, contacted me. She was scheduled to be released from her latest prison stay and needed a place to be paroled to. She asked me if she could come to our home. We had a second bedroom, so I asked the guy I was taking care of what he thought and, of course, he agreed. Why wouldn't he? It wouldn't change anything for him. He wasn't paying even one bill anyway.

Lynn showed up and immediately made herself at home. Now I was taking care of two adults. I'd leave them at home every morning and return in the evening hungry and spent, to nothing but a garbage can full of fast-food wrappers. Usually the two of them were chilling, laughing and talking together like it was normal that I was the only one working.

Lynn seemed to unleash some bold gene in Tony and he stopped trying to hide the fact that he smoked crack from me. He and Lynn smoked together, from what I could tell, every day. Lynn even smoked in my presence and talked about her addiction. I asked her not to do that in my home because I was concerned about Tony doing it, too. She said she'd "try," but it was hard to quit and that if he really wanted to smoke, it wouldn't matter what she did anyway. What had I gotten myself into and why didn't I put a stop to it right then?

When I agreed that Lynn could be paroled to me, I told her she could only stay three months because I was newly married and didn't think it was a great idea for her to be there too long. She agreed, but the three-month mark passed, as did months four and five, without any hint that she was ready to go anywhere.

"Lynn," I said one evening after a long day of customer sales calls, "we agreed you'd only be here three months; it's been almost six. What's up?"

"Damn, Ang!" she exclaimed. "What's the big deal? It's not like you don't have the space! I would do it for you."

"That's not the point," I responded. "We had an agreement that you're just ignoring. And we don't know if you'd do it for me. You're always on the receiving end of a favor. I need you to find someplace else to go by the end of the month."

"Yeah, okay, whatever," she said with an attitude. "You think you all that cause you got a house," she snorted as she walked out of the kitchen, *my* kitchen, and back to the bedroom, *my* spare room, in *my* house, and slammed *my* door.

Whatever, I thought. Just get your ass outta my house by the end of the month!

A few days later, I left work early and as I turned the key in the lock at home, I could hear what sounded like scurrying feet and loud whispers. I opened the door to Lynn heading back to her room in nothing but her bra and panties.

"What's going on, Lynn?" I said, trying to keep my cool. "Where's Tony? Why are you walking around half-naked?"

118

"I think he's in the living room," she responded, trying to sound casual. "I just went to get a drink of water. I haven't been walking around him like this."

"You know what?" I said, getting angrier by the moment. "You gotta go! For you to leave your room *ever* half-dressed like that, knowing my husband is here, is *so* disrespectful! I shouldn't have to tell you that!"

"You trippin'!" she responded. "It's not a big deal. He didn't even see me! I told you I'd be out in a couple of weeks."

"Nah, fuck that!" I snapped. "You need to be outta here by tomorrow. I'm serious. You the one trippin'!"

"What's up?" Tony said as he appeared from the living room. "Why she gotta go?"

I looked at him like his devil's horns were actually suddenly visible.

"What do you mean, why she gotta go? Because she has no respect, and you must not either if you think it's okay for her to stay here."

"Aw, it ain't no big deal," he said as he moved in to kiss me. "She can stay. I didn't see anything. Lynn, go put on some clothes so we can all talk."

I moved away from him, avoiding his touch, and glared at Lynn's back as she moved to the bedroom.

"You know what?" I said as I turned back to Tony. "Something's not right. I know it and you both know I know it. She's gotta go and if you want to, you can go with her."

"Well, I guess she's gotta go, then, cause you *know* I ain't going nowhere," he said as he turned on his heel, went into our room, and closed the door.

I took the next day off and woke up telling Lynn to do whatever she had to do, but she was leaving my house *that* day. She made a few phone calls and by early that afternoon she had a friend there to pick her up.

"You still a bitch, I see," she said as she packed a bag.

"Girl, whatever. Just as long as you get your ass outta my house, I don't care what you think," I responded.

"I'll be back to get the rest of my things," she said.

"Nah, you're taking all this shit with you today. And don't worry about giving me my key back. I'm changing the locks today, too." I went into the kitchen and got a box of garbage bags for her to put the rest of her things in.

She snatched it from me and started stuffing her clothes in a bag.

"Let me help you," I said. "I don't want you to leave anything here. You don't need a reason to come back."

Tony just stood there, looking stupid, like he wanted to say something but thought better of it.

I am 100 percent certain they had sex. The combination of the drug abuse and the sexual proclivities of the two of them leaves no doubt in my mind that I walked in that day on something that was either about to start or was already over, and that wasn't the first time.

A few years later, we started hanging out again. For some reason, I was crazy about Lynn and I wanted us to be close. She was brilliant; we challenged each other to think deeply and we had countless thoughtful conversations. I really tried to make our relationship work, and I think for a while she did, too, but I still put up with too much of her nonsense. I wish I could say I jumped, but eventually she pushed me off the crazy-go-round that was our relationship with her selfish, dishonest, and abusive behavior and words and I chose not to ride again.

Another of the many stupid mistakes I made in this sham of a marriage was to agree to a joint checking account that all of our money would go into. The trouble was that 98 percent of the money going in was mine. I paid all the bills from that account and we both used it for our expenses.

"Tony, I just got a notice from the bank saying all the checks I wrote for bills last week have bounced!" I almost shouted when he walked in one evening, obviously high. The amount of money he'd been taking from the account had begun to escalate over the last several months, but I always had enough to cover the mortgage and other bills, with some left over. Plus, he claimed every time that he'd withdrawn the money for gas or some other legitimate expense and that he would replace it "by the end of the week, when he got his check" or "in a few days, when so-and-so paid him back." This time was no different.

"Yeah, I needed it. I'll put it back. What's the big deal, anyway? Why don't you just take it out of your savings? I know you have a savings account separate from me. Use that."

"Really?" I asked. "Use that? I shouldn't have to 'use that.' You should stop putting our bill money in that pipe and get a job!"

"You trippin'! I said I'd put it back! I'm sleepy. Good night," he said as he brushed past me and walked into the bedroom, clearly done with our "conversation."

He didn't put the money back and I tapped my savings to cover all the bounced checks and the fees.

Two weeks later, it happened again. I finally got the message, opened a separate checking account and changed my direct deposit from work to this account. When he realized there was no more money going into the account for him to use, he snapped!

"So, what am I supposed to do for money?" he yelled as he walked through the door one evening. "How do you expect me to get back and forth to work?"

I was at the sink, peeling potatoes for dinner, and he was standing way too close and talking far too loud for me to think this was going to be a reasonable conversation. His eyes were glassy. It was clear he'd been getting high.

"Well, hi to you, too. Can you give me some space, please? What are you talking about?" I asked as innocently as I could.

"You know damn well what I'm talking about! I went to get some money out of our account today and there wasn't any there. They told me there were no direct deposits set up for this account! Why did you change it?" His voice was getting louder and deeper at the same time.

"Why did I change it? You're joking, right? You know why I changed it! How do you expect me to pay the mortgage and everything else if you're just gonna take *my* money out of the bank before I can? You acting like it's *your money*! Damn! Why don't you take your ass to work?"

He must have been looking for any reason to hit me because that's just what he did.

"Bitch!" he said as he took a step back and slapped me hard across the face. "Why you always gotta talk shit? Just give me twenty dollars! Where are your car keys?"

I stood there glaring at him, with one hand on my face and the other clenching the knife I was peeling potatoes with, trying to decide if I was gonna stab him in the eye.

"What? You wanna hit me back? Go ahead, I'll knock your ass out!"

We stood there, eyeball to eyeball, neither of us flinching, while I willed myself not to cry.

"Yeah, that's what I thought," he said after about a minute.

He turned and walked out of the kitchen while I stood at the sink, more mad than hurt, thinking about how I was gonna get away from this monster.

A minute later, he called from the front hallway, "I only took fifty outta your purse!" Then I heard the front door slam.

I went to the bedroom to check my purse. Not only had he taken my money, but he also had my car keys.

Hours later, he still wasn't back. I walked several blocks to a place where I knew he hung out to get high and, yep, my car was parked a few doors down. I used my spare key and drove back home.

This wasn't the first time he'd hit me, nor would it be the last. This insane behavior continued for months. He'd demand money and my car. We'd argue and fight. The neighbors complained. The police were called. They showed up and were useless, telling us to keep it down and for him to "relax."

Random act of kindness

I was frustrated and emotionally exhausted. So often, when I felt like I couldn't take another step, an angel appeared in my path to ease my way. Once, when I was particularly down, tears streaked my face as I walked past a building toward the lake a couple of blocks from our condo. I was headed there to take a walk and try to clear my head. A pretty woman with sunshine for a smile stopped me.

"What's wrong, sweetie-pea? Do you need anything?" she asked.

"No, I'm okay," I responded. "I just need a walk."

"Come sit down for a minute. Do you want to talk?" she asked as she pointed to a nearby bench and gently took my arm, guiding me to sit down. The minute I sat down, I started to cry harder. She held my hands and waited for me to catch my breath.

"I apologize!" I said. I don't even know you, and here I am crying on your shoulder!"

She laughed, still holding my hands. "My name is Peaches and you don't owe me an apology! I stopped you! I want to make sure you're okay."

Just her voice and the kindness in her eyes made me feel better. I thank God for the "coincidence" of our meeting that day. I spent many hours at her condo, talking, laughing, and, yes, crying as I walked through that hell. All these years later, we're still great friends.

"Running away. Leaving a bad situation." Maze, Featuring Frankie Beverly

I kept working and paying the bills, all the while plotting my getaway.

Finally, I saw my chance! His uncle passed in a city a few hours away and the funeral was scheduled for a Thursday. I put a few friends on notice and told him I couldn't attend because I had to work. His family picked him up around seven that morning and I waved from the window as he got into the car. I dialed my friends while I watched them pull away, and then I sprang into action, throwing clothes, shoes, and books into garbage bags and stacking them at the back door.

I had another friend, Anita, who generously offered to let me escape to the house she'd recently vacated a little farther south from where we lived in Hyde Park.

I called the phone company and scheduled to have the phone service transferred from my home to my refuge. I told them I was escaping a domestic violence situation and to please keep my forwarding address private. The representative told me she was flagging my account so no other agents would give out any information without a code.

My friends showed up and we packed their cars and mine with everything important to me.

I locked the door to the home I loved for the last time. "Just bricks and mortar," I said, and headed south to what I hoped would be a new beginning.

My friends, Derrick and Roxie, helped unload the cars before they headed back to work and left me alone to get my head around what was happening.

I think I did more crying than organizing and the day quickly dissolved into night. I was jumpy and couldn't sleep, so I called yet another friend, Michelle, to ask if I could spend the night at her house. Of course she agreed, and I grabbed a bag and headed over there, where I cried some more and wondered out loud how in the world I'd ended up here at only twenty-four.

The next morning, I went back to my new home and found that it had been broken into, my things thrown all over the place, and many of my favorite possessions—artwork, books, etc.—either missing or trashed. While I was assessing the damage, the phone rang. I was shocked to hear his voice on the other end.

"Don't you know you can't get away from me? There's nowhere you can go that I won't find you. How dare you try to leave me! You must be out of your motherfuckin' mind! I guess I shoulda done a better job of beatin' yo' ass to get my point across!" Tony yelled into the phone.

I was petrified! How had he found me? I'd suspected it, but now I was certain it was him who'd broken into my house overnight. I didn't think it then, but this was yet another time when my angels were watching over me. What if I had been there when he came? What might he have done? I was panic-stricken and hyperventilating from fear. I hung up and peeked out the window. Was he somehow watching me even then? How did he know I was back home? I grabbed the same bag I'd taken the night before and ran out of the house and back to my friend's. Once there, I called the phone company to find out what had happened. It turned out he'd called and because he had all the right identifying information, when he told them he'd had the phone number changed to a new address, but couldn't remember the exact address, they'd given it to him even though I'd clearly stated that I was running from a domestic violence situation! I should have sued! Their actions could have led to me being beaten or worse. As it was, my being robbed, threatened, and further traumatized was a direct result of their lack of diligence.

I was so shaken that I immediately called my mom. After I told her what had happened, she insisted I come home right away. I repacked my bag and headed to Rockford. I spent most of the weekend crying on her shoulder, receiving her love and encouragement, and eating as much of her good food as I could, given the circumstances.

Bowed but not yet broken

On Sunday, although I was still shaken and upset, I knew I had to head back to Chicago so I could go to work the next day. My younger brother was able to take a few days off and he offered to come back with me so I wouldn't be alone. We arrived late that evening and stayed up talking through most of the night, finally nodding off sometime after 4:00 a.m. A couple of hours later, I was up again. I dressed for work then woke my brother up to tell him I was leaving. I went outside to my car to find *it* vandalized! All of my car's windows were busted, the dashboard was smashed, and the radio was missing. It also sat on four flats. I ran back into the house, crying and screaming for my brother.

"Ang, what's wrong? What happened?" he said, panicked by my hysterics.

I sobbed out what had happened as he held me and told me everything would be okay and he wouldn't let anything happen to me.

In one short weekend, I'd been robbed, threatened, stalked, and terrorized. I may have been shaken to my core, but I'm tough, like my mom. Things have to be *really* bad for me to miss work. I got myself together, got on the bus, and headed downtown for a day of meetings, proposal writing, product demonstrations, and customer visits.

By the time I got back south, because it was October, it was already dusk. I was dismayed to see that my car was exactly as I'd left it that morning. My brother had straightened up the mess "Terrible Tony" had left, throwing away what wasn't salvageable and stacking what he knew I'd want to inspect. While I really appreciated his efforts, in my fragile state, I was focused on what *wasn't* done. When I asked him why he hadn't cleaned up the broken glass or done anything to help me with my car, he said that all our lives I'd been so particular about everything and so independent that he didn't think I'd want his help. When he'd tried to help me earlier that morning, I'd snapped at him out of pain, fear, and exhaustion. His response spoke volumes to me about myself, about our relationship, and about how my being "strong" and stepping in to fill what I thought was a void left by our mom working and our dad's incarceration hadn't gone over too well.

Exhausted from the emotional and psychological stress and my workday, I dug deeper, called the police, and filed a report. Then my brother and I went back outside to clean up the damage done to my car before I prepared for work the next day. My brother stayed with me for the rest of the week, which I greatly appreciated, but I still felt vulnerable. I felt that he'd shown me he couldn't protect me—even though I was pushing him away. In retrospect, I know it wasn't fair to be so hard on him. He did a lot inside the house and his explanation for why he hadn't touched my car made sense. To expect him to be able to protect me was unreasonable. He was, after all, only nineteen and he'd never seen a man be a man. The fallout from Daddy's incarceration and resulting rage continued. Age five was the last time I'd felt truly loved and protected by any man, and my brother's lack of action and inability to calm me only served to reinforce the feeling. Our father, and by extension, the broken penal system, had failed and wounded him, too.

It was then that I carried you

As I look back on my life, I'm awed by God's grace and the constant presence of earthly angels sent to protect me and smooth my way. A few weeks before I fled my marriage, I had called my childhood friend, who owned an insurance agency franchise. When I told Wayne what was going on, he insisted that he write a renter's policy for me that he paid the deposit on. "Just in case," he said. This policy came in handy when I needed to replace some of the items Tony stole and repair the damage he caused to my friend's home.

The next day at work, I shared my woes with a coworker, an older black man with whom I'd shared many conversations over the years. He told me I needed protection. He said he had a .22 I could borrow and he would show me how to use it carefully. He did just that.

At the end of the week, with my car repaired, I took my brother back home to Rockford. When I returned, I "slept" sitting up, facing the door, with the gun in my lap. Needless to say, I awoke exhausted both physically and mentally. This went on for a few weeks. I'd had my number changed, but before long, the phone started ringing at all hours of the night. When I answered, there was nothing but silence on the other end. I was absolutely petrified, but I told few people. Who would understand? Who would care? Who would help?

I devised a plan to pack an overnight bag and leave it in my trunk. I worked all day at Xerox and when everybody else left for the day, I claimed I needed to stay late to work on proposals. This wasn't unusual; I'd built my career on coming in early and leaving late. It's how I stayed near the top of the pack and made President's Club year after year. In fact, many nights half the team was there late, strategizing, writing proposals, and eating pizza. If it weren't for all the drama at home, it would count as one of the most energized, enjoyable times of my work life.

Because everyone was accustomed to arriving early, staying late, and working weekends, nobody questioned me. When I was sure everyone was gone, I'd go get my bag from my car, go into one of the lounges, and sleep for a few hours. I'd awaken early before anyone started arriving for work, wash up, put on fresh clothes, take my bag back to my car, and be sitting at my desk as if I'd just arrived early when my coworkers got there. When we all hit the streets for our territories and a day of selling, I'd head south. It felt so much safer being in the house for a few minutes in the middle of the day, so I'd go back "home" to pack fresh clothes, soap, deodorant, toothbrush and paste, makeup, etc., then start a load of laundry and rush back downtown to work a full day.

Other times, when I just couldn't sleep at all, I'd wait until the sun was just coming up and head back to the house then, still making it back to the office before anyone else had arrived. I thought it made sense to switch up my visits to the house—if he was watching, he wouldn't be able to pin down a schedule. This was fine for a few weeks, but I was starting to fray around the edges. I was always on high alert. Worrying that I was being followed and wondering when he might jump out of a shadow or be in the house when I arrived was stressful. Keeping my sales numbers up, keeping up with the required daily reports, proposals, meetings, time sheets, expense reports, customer calls, follow-up appointments, and everything else it took to do my job was also taking its toll. I wasn't eating and was barely sleeping (I didn't want to get caught living at the office!), and I looked like it.

One evening, as I sat with my HVME—high-volume marketing executive—Lisa, working on a major proposal for a big customer, my mind wandered.

"Angel, what's wrong with you? Why aren't you paying attention?" Lisa practically bellowed.

"Oh, I—I apologize," I stammered. "I didn't sleep well last night."

"Well, that's not my problem. We've gotta get this proposal right before our appointment in the morning!" She sat there, literally picking her nose and sticking her fingers in her mouth, as she punched the calculator keys with her free hand.

"You're right," I agreed, trying to ignore her nasty habit as I pushed my chair back from her a bit so she wouldn't get any boogers on me. I guess we all have our own ways of dealing with stress, I thought.

She just wouldn't let it go, though. "This is *your* customer, too! Not just mine. If you don't help me get this right, I'm gonna have to tell your manager that you're not pulling your weight!"

I couldn't hold back the tears anymore and I got up and headed for the bathroom without another word. I closed the stall door behind me and silently cried a river.

"Angel, are you okay? What's going on?" Lisa asked from the other side of the stall door. "Are you crying?!"

"No, no, I'm good. I just needed to blow my nose. I'll be out in a minute," I responded.

"Okaaay, if you're sure . . .? You know you can talk to me if you need to, right?" she asked.

"Nah, seriously, I'm good. Go on back to your desk. I'll be there in a minute."

I wouldn't share the time of day with you if you were the last soul on the planet, I thought. Telling Lisa my business would have been like announcing it on the intercom system to the entire office.

I took a few deep breaths, said a short prayer, and washed my face before heading back to our workspace to finish the proposal. I'm strong, like my mom, I said to myself. I can do this. And I did.

Several weeks into this "growth experience," my checks started bouncing again. What now? I thought. When I went to the bank to figure out what was going on, I found out that my con-artist ex had added check buster to his long list of "accomplishments." It seems that when he'd broken into my new place, he'd taken a book of checks and wrote checks to himself and others to the tune of more than $10,000. This time, filing criminal charges against him for his dirty deeds was out of my hands. This common criminal had committed bank fraud, a federal crime, and they planned to make him pay.

One day as I was heading back to the office, just as the sun was coming up, one of the janitors, a Haitian man with beautiful dark chocolate skin and eerie bright-blue eyes, came running up to me.

"Angel, are you okay? I had a dream that a man was stalking you, came out of the shadows of a building when you were on your way here, and shot you in the street! I thought you were dead!"

I looked at him like he'd lost his mind! Sure, we talked all the time and I knew about his life back in Haiti, some of his beliefs, and the fact that he was a "seer," but he didn't know what was going on with me.

I was careful not to tell anyone how bad things really were. I didn't want people judging me, feeling sorry for me, or spreading my business and talking about me. I also didn't want my situation to affect my job. I needed to keep working! So, when he said this to me, I just lost it. I started hyperventilating and crying almost uncontrollably. I had been frightened before, but now I was petrified! Had he seen my future?

I went to a phone, called in sick, went back to my car, and drove to my aunt and uncle's house on the south side, where I'd been living when I met my stalker-ex. When my aunt opened the door, I literally collapsed into her arms. I was barely coherent as I tried to tell her everything that had been going on with me over the last several months. She just held me and listened. When I finally finished, she began to pray over me, holding me and telling me everything was going to be okay. I stayed with them for a few days just to come up with a plan for what to do next.

God's grace was always with me. I began looking for apartments in Hyde Park. I found a beautiful apartment in a building that was fully occupied but, by the grace of God, the current renter needed to sublet. Not only did I get the unit at a discount, but she left some of her furniture, so I didn't have to completely start over! She also had a beautiful Siamese seal point kitten that she couldn't take with her and asked me if I was willing to keep it. I'd never had a cat, but it was so cute and it was company! I said yes. I fell in love with Sunset immediately and she slept with me every night as my new best friend!

Several times, I went back to the condo to discuss our impending divorce or to ask Tony, or DT as I'd started to think of him, which is short for "Demon Tony," to move since he wasn't paying any of the bills anyway and never had. The electricity was off and he was stealing electricity from the hallway. There were cords running from the hallway throughout the house to lamps, the TV, etc. He was no longer hiding the fact that he smoked crack. The house reeked of the sickly sweet smell and another odor—sex? Yeah, he'd turned my beautiful home into a drug and sex den. I'd hooked up with the real devil.

He was absolutely uncooperative. No to everything. No to the divorce. No to moving out so I could move back in and save what I'd worked so hard for. No to paying any bills so my credit might be salvaged. Just no, no, no.

Once, as I was leaving, he got in the elevator with me, waited for the door to close, and put his hands around my neck, choking my air off so I couldn't breathe or talk. He told me I needed to recognize that I was his and he wasn't ready to let me go. He said he could "have me" anytime he wanted and if I knew what was good for me I'd return "home." He loosened his grip just as the elevator doors opened into the lobby. He kissed me, smiled, and said "I love you. Glad you came by. You be safe getting home." Then he turned to the doorman and winked. I was gasping for air and trying not to show my utter terror. I ran out of the elevator past the doorman whom I'd known for years and thought of as a friend without saying a word. When I got to my car, I again collapsed into tears. After a few minutes, I got myself together enough to drive to my new apartment, which I felt was a safe haven.

Showtime!

I tried hard to appreciate the good. My location was great. The bus to take me downtown to work was right outside my door and the ride was only twenty minutes. I felt really blessed to have landed "softly" in this space. I was starting to get my mojo back at work, too. I started to close more sales and make more money. President's Club was again within striking distance.

Even as things were getting better, I was still going through the divorce and losing the condo I'd purchased to foreclosure (neither the mortgage nor HOA dues were being paid). DT continued to live there in the dark, not paying a single bill. He called me almost daily, alternating between begging and threatening me to "come back home." I felt confident that he didn't know I lived about four blocks from him because I was able to keep the same phone number, and this time I had elevated my complaint and concern to the phone company management to not share my private information with anyone, with the threat of a lawsuit if they did!

I could usually put on a happy face, but my heart was heavy from years of unresolved trauma, abuse, disappointment, and fear. At the same time all of this was going on, I began to have severe pain and profuse bleeding every time I used the bathroom. The pain was so great that I ate very little, hoping I wouldn't have to go as often. When I did have to go, I held it as long as I could to keep the pain at bay. All the blood in the toilet scared me, too. After several doctor's visits, I learned the cause: I had many massive uterine fibroids that were pushing on various organs, including my rectum. They were too large to remove without a hysterectomy and I still very much wanted children. The doctor prescribed a drug to help shrink them so they could be surgically removed while leaving my uterus intact. I was unaware that a side effect of this drug was depression. I was already depressed, but this drug took me to a new low. I became suicidal.

In the midst of all this, our sales team got a new manager. Anita Gomez was the most insecure, incompetent, unpleasant person I'd ever worked with. We clashed from day one. Although I continued to work hard, delivered good sales numbers and stayed on top of all of my responsibilities, she worked just as hard to find fault in everything I did. When she called me into her office one day to go over our upcoming travel day, I told her we'd need to plan a little differently because I was unable to walk long distances due to the pain the fibroids were causing.

"We'll have to see customers within a few blocks of the office, so I can walk there or schedule fewer appointments so we'll have the time to take a cab," I told her during our strategy session.

"If you're in that much pain, why don't you just quit?!" she demanded, her face twisted into its usual snarl.

"Anita, that's ridiculous," I responded. "If I quit, I won't have insurance to get the care I need to get better."

"Well, that's not my problem. You need to figure something out. If you can't do everything the job requires, then you can't keep the job."

"I *am* doing everything the job requires," I retorted. "I didn't say I couldn't see customers, I just said we had to plan to accommodate my inability to walk long distances."

"Angel, just figure it out and keep your customer calls up. I have another meeting. I'll meet you here at 8am so we can leave together for our first call." She stood up, indicating that our meeting was over.

Without another word, I picked up my planner and left her office.

Because I controlled the schedule, I made all of our calls close to the office so that we could walk. I couldn't walk fast because of the pain and she couldn't walk fast because she insisted on wearing four inch heels even on travel days. Even with my slow pace due to my discomfort, Anita had a hard time keeping up with me. It was hard not to laugh as I watched her hobble down the street, thinking she was cute.

During each visit, instead of presenting to the customers together as a team, the way I had with every other manager, Anita just sat in stony silence, glaring at me as I made my presentations. When I attempted to include her in the conversation, she actually said "this is your call. You know best what they need." I knew she was incompetent. She knew she was incompetent and now the customer knew it, too.

I cried all the time! I pulled myself together anytime I needed to interact with people: at work, on the bus going to work, or any other time people were around. The minute I was alone, the tears rushed to my eyes again. The minute I got home, I locked the door and didn't come out until it was time to go to work the next morning.

I began to think of ways I could stop the pain and emotional exhaustion forever. Even when I thought of my beautiful mom and

133

how upset she would be if I took my life, it wasn't enough to make me stop thinking this way.

What *did* stop me from following through on my plans and desires was my belief that God wouldn't forgive me if I committed this final act. Instead, I hoped a bus would jump a curb and do the deed for me. This pain and these thoughts lasted for months. I told my mom and my sister, and they stepped in as my prayer warriors and called me daily to check on me and lift me up. Many times when I talked to my mom on the phone, I just cried, often uncontrollably.

"Oh, honey, I'm here," she'd say every now and then. She never rushed me or made me feel silly or guilty for what I was going through. When I finally calmed down, she prayed for me, told me how much she loved me, and promised me that everything was going to be okay before we signed off.

My mother and sister's intercession during that time saved my life and kept that bus from jumping the curb!

Acts from the depths of pain

One evening as I exited the bus right outside my apartment building, *he* stepped out of the shadows.

"Hi," he said.

Scared me to death! "Get away from me!" I screamed. "What do you want?"

"Whoa! Relax! I'm not going to hurt you," DT responded. "I missed you and I want us to try again."

How had this gremlin found me? How could this be happening again? The cocoon of safety I'd created was shattered.

He told me they'd padlocked the condo and he had nowhere to go. Could he stay with me just for a few days while he found someplace else to go?

"No! Hell, no! Get the fuck away from me!" I shouted. "I can't believe you'd ask me that after all you've done to me!"

"Okay, okay. I didn't mean to scare you. I just miss you and I thought I could stay here for a while. I'll go."

I watched him walk off into the night, shaken by the fact that he not only knew where I lived, but had an idea of my schedule.

Over the next few weeks, he showed up again and again, sometimes with flowers, always with a big smile and a sad story.

"Please let me stay with you, just for a few days. I want to show you I've changed. I think we can work it out. I don't have anyplace else to go."

Go back to the hole you crawled out of to come stalk and harass me, I wanted to say.

"Why can't you give us one more chance?"

To this day, I honestly don't know how he wormed himself back into my house. Not my heart, but my house. Profound depression, I guess. As winter set in, I unbelievably softened and didn't want to see him out in the cold. I told him he could stay just for a few days until he got himself together. This was absolutely ridiculous! His father was an assistant principal at Percy Julian High School. His mom was an elementary school teacher and his only sibling, his younger sister, was in med school! He didn't need to stay with me. He was the only unstable member of his family. He was twelve years older than me and the same manipulative devil he'd always been. I was in my early twenties and the walking wounded. I had no idea how to protect myself from manipulation or abuse.

He moved in and slept on the couch. I didn't give him a key but, crazy as it sounds, I did sometimes leave him in the house when I went to work. He kept trying to get back with me, trying to climb into bed with me. I kept telling him absolutely not, that his being there was a favor and should not been seen in any way as an indication that we might get back together. When this truth finally began to set in for him, he got nasty again. The arguing and name-calling started again. I kept telling him he had to go, and he had the nerve to tell me he wasn't leaving until *he* was ready to go.

I came home one day to my house torn up a bit. Drawers were pulled out with the contents dumped on the floor. The bed was pulled apart and sofa cushions were on the floor. What was he looking for? Something he could steal and sell? At least I had enough sense to not leave anything of value there while I was away. My cat, Sunset, was hiding under the bed. I had to coax her out. Thankfully, she wasn't hurt.

I immediately called the police, notified management that he must not be allowed back in, and changed the locks. I packed the few things he had there and took them to his parents' house. I told them that he wasn't welcome in my home again and that, along with the outstanding check charges against him, I'd filed charges for harassment and vandalism.

Once again, I had to regroup and find my peace. Fortunately, my divorce was final shortly thereafter. He was eventually arrested, but his family bailed him out and spent enough money to buy him a slap on the wrist. He finally left me alone, and a couple of years later, his sister called to tell me he'd finally messed with the wrong person, who responded with a shot to the middle of his chest. I went to the funeral home to make sure it was him so I could finally close that chapter of my life for good.

"Goodbye and good riddance! Answer to God for all the horror you spilled into the world! I know He forgives you and I'm working on it, but I can't say I'm sad that you're gone," I said quietly as I looked at him in his casket.

Fact: Suicide is the second leading cause of death in people ages 10 to 34 and the fourth leading cause of death among people ages 35 to 54. There were two and a half times more suicide deaths than homicides in 2018. Women are more likely to attempt suicide than men, but are less likely to die this way, in large part because of the methods they choose.

Call to Action: If you are having suicidal thoughts, contact the National Suicide Prevention Lifeline at 1-800-273-8255 for support and assistance from a trained counselor.

Please see *Healing Waters: The Workbook* for other resources and articles on suicide.

Fact: Every day in America, three women are killed by their mates, who are usually men.

Call to Action: Domestic violence is *never* okay. If you are being abused or know someone who is, seek help or offer help. Please refer to *Healing Waters: The Workbook* for more complete coverage of this topic, including tips and resources on how to remove yourself from violent situations.

Chapter 18

Falling Forward

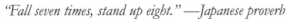

"Fall seven times, stand up eight." —*Japanese proverb*

I was still excited about real estate, so I saved every penny and soon bought my first two-unit building. Then I bought another one, and another. After a lot of hard work and sacrifice, some favor, and being in the right places at the right times, I eventually owned about sixty units.

I was back in touch with Lynn and she asked me to front for her in the purchase of a building. Still vulnerable and wanting, for some crazy reason, to maintain a relationship with her, I agreed. She provided the down payment from funds she'd accumulated while "coloring outside the lines" and "we" bought a building that was in my name only. Before long, she found herself back in prison and I was left to handle all of my buildings along with the tenants, maintenance, upkeep, and mortgage on hers.

While she was locked up, she continued to ask me to do her big favors. She asked me to go to certain pharmacies and purchase "cut" for her "coworkers," then leave it in her apartment for them to pick up later. (We kept one of the five units as her own.) Clearly, Lynn and I thought the same of me—not very highly. She asked me to jeopardize my freedom by engaging in her illegal activities. I, thinking I was helping her, put her selfish needs before my own and did as she asked. Even this wasn't enough to buy her love and loyalty. At some point she decided I wasn't handling things to her liking and she began writing me horrible letters, telling me how much she'd always hated me and my mom, that I'd better not lose her building while she was locked up, and that one day, before I could see it coming, she was going to kill me.

Once again, I found myself looking over my shoulder and sleeping with one eye open because someone I'd loved was plotting my demise.

When she was released, for the first time in her crime-ridden life, she came home to a place she could call her own. She had steady, legal income and considerable equity in a building that she'd done next to nothing to create, maintain, or protect.

Instead of being appreciative, she snatched her keys and said, "Get my building out of your name, bitch!"

I happily quit-claimed the building to her and vowed not to let her hurt me again. It came as no surprise that she was unable to hold onto it for very long.

Several more years passed before we saw each other again at a family member's funeral. We were cordial, but I was finally, happily, gratefully done with her and I never looked back.

◆———————————◉———————————◆

Fact: We teach people how to treat us. Respect and self-esteem are an inside job. As Dr. King put it, "A man can't ride your back unless it's bent."

◆———————————◉———————————◆

Call to Action: Loving ourselves fully takes work and practice, but it's so worth it!

Please see *Healing Waters: The Workbook* for an abundance of exercises, information, and resources about how to build or rebuild tattered self-esteem and fall in love with yourself!

Chapter 19

Wake Up!

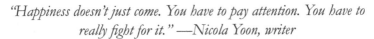

"Happiness doesn't just come. You have to pay attention. You have to really fight for it." —Nicola Yoon, writer

Even as I continued to subject myself to nonsense, my family and I remained close. I spent weekends in Rockford regularly and both my siblings and my parents came to visit and spend weekends with me. Sometimes they came individually and sometimes they all came together. Almost every weekend, I was with family.

These times and memories are mostly good and certainly ones that I will always cherish because they gave us beautiful bonding and healing time.

I say "mostly good" because I admit that I was a member of the Walking Wounded Club, and it's hard to bleed from unhealed lacerations and not get that blood on anybody who dares to get close.

My brother Dean came many times other than the week he stayed to comfort and protect me when I first separated from DT. We just hung out, walking along the lake or going to museums, getting to know each other better, and having a good time.

My dad came, too. He would spend a week or more at a time with me when he was between jobs. We talked almost nonstop when I wasn't at work and I was able to ask him many of the questions that burned inside me about why he inflicted so much pain and what his life was like while he was incarcerated. I didn't get all my questions answered and I remained unsatisfied with some of his responses, but I'm grateful for the time we spent together and the efforts we made to heal.

My mom and Deb came most often, though, and usually separately.

My sister and I agreed that we were committed to being close and growing our relationship beyond blood to a real friendship, so she spent one weekend most months with me in Chicago. I always tried to have something planned and we went to plays, museums, motivational talks, and church. In between, we took long walks by the lake or sat up late at night eating cheese and caramel mixed popcorn, laughing, and talking. Sometimes, though, a "pain demon" would rear its ugly head and I'd get into a funk or become angry about less than nothing. During these times, instead of packing her bag and heading to her car in a huff, Deb would retreat to my bedroom with a magazine to wait out my venture into "Nellie's Room." When we were kids, we'd say anyone who was trippin' about nothing was "in Nellie's Room" before bursting out into uncontrollable laughter. I have no idea how we came up with that or why we thought it was so funny, except to say that we are our mother's children and we, like her, often use humor to lighten a mood.

My mom came just as much as my sister did, and we, too, had some fabulous visits. I relished the opportunity to take her to nice restaurants, clothing stores, great plays, and all the cultural events Chicago has to offer. It was my honor to try to give her back just a bit of all she's poured into me my entire life. Sometimes I'd get moody when mom and I were hanging out together, but not as much as when Deb came. Maybe it was because Mom is *Mom* and out of respect, I kept myself in check. Whatever the reason, I'll be forever grateful to my entire family for hanging in there with me, being committed to our relationships and the bigger picture. It would be untrue to say we haven't all hit bumps, some considerable, along the way, but our commitment to each other hasn't wavered and we continue to have honest, sometimes hard conversations that keep us moving forward.

Still, I continued to drift from one unpleasant relationship to another.

For several years, the abuse continued. I was hit, choked, cursed out, lied to, lied about, taken advantage of, embarrassed, disrespected, disregarded, cheated financially, and cheated on sexually and emotionally. I was physically, mentally, and emotionally exhausted.

Don't believe the lies, Angel

This habit of "cutting myself" that I'd learned as a child continued. I didn't literally cut myself, but I saw the way I accepted abuse from myself and others as a cutting of my soul. Accepting and participating in these experiences reinforced that nagging voice I still heard.

"People don't really like you."

"You'll never find a good man to love you."

"You're not pretty enough."

Blah, blah, blah. All of these were variations of what I'd learned as a child: the feelings of abandonment, the belief that abuse was okay, and the acceptance of self-sacrifice as not only okay, but expected.

Exploitation by any other name is still exploitation

Even though I was in emotional pain, I still believed healing and peace were possible. I still prayed all the time, but going to church? Not so much. I was disillusioned by my early experience in Chicago with being asked repeatedly for money, then being guilted into giving even more with the use of scripture: *"Will a man rob God? Yet you are robbing me. But you say, 'How have we robbed you?' In your tithes and offerings"* (Malachi 3:8).

To me, that's no way to raise an offering or encourage church members to build loving, trusting relationships with God, with Jehovah Jireh, Who loves us and wants to provide for us. But that's the way the pastor of the church I'd turned to for comfort during some of my most challenging times raised his offering. I gave all I could, too. After the first offering was raised, the deacons would come back and whisper in the pastor's ear, and he'd start the offering process all over again. This time, though, he boldly called out congregants by name!

"We're still short this evening, family," he'd say. "Who's willing to dig deep and give a little more for God's work? Angel, I know you have another twenty dollars for the offering. And what about you, Sister Smith? Come on, let's be obedient to the Lord. I'm going to start us off with another fifty dollars from my own pocket."

143

Wait a minute, I thought. You probably just took that out of the offering plate to put it right back in! That was what I *thought,* but what I did was dutifully go back into my purse to retrieve my lunch money or bus fare for the rest of the week and make my way back down the aisle to drop it in the offering plate.

If this is what it takes to be in God's will and be free of all this pain and heartache I'm carrying, it's worth it, I said to myself.

Sometimes I'd leave church with nothing but lint in my pocket, and for the most part I was okay with that. I might still be there had he or any of his members shown up just once when I cried out for help or missed several services in a row. While he knew my name when it came time to collect the offering, I was a distant memory when I wasn't there.

So church, for me, was a disappointment. I missed the fellowship I'd grown up with at our church in Rockford, but I felt I'd outgrown some of the beliefs taught by my childhood denomination. So inwardly, I asked for guidance. I knew there had to be a place that spoke to the emotional, spiritual, and financial freedom that I believed was available to me and that I deserved. I asked for clear signs to lead me to that place. They came in the form of repeated conversations and bumper stickers (yep, bumper stickers!) that seemed to be everywhere!

Finally, a spiritual breath of fresh air

Fortunately, I was listening, and I found myself pulling into the parking lot of one of the largest New Thought churches on Chicago's south side. When I walked in, I felt like I was home. Hearing the female pastor, the Reverend Dr. Johnnie Colemon, teach that God's goodness and health, wholeness, peace, and prosperity were my birthright was new to my ears, but not to my heart. I practically ran to church every Sunday to soak up the teachings and I began to see the Bible differently. Now, the same scriptures I'd read about God's promises took on new meaning and I got confirmation of what I'd believed in my heart, that God wanted *me* to be happy and whole, too. That God loves me, protects me, and wants to be in relationship with me. Now, I wasn't just reading my Bible; I was in class, learning to study it. I was meditating on it and how it applied to me and my life. I was earnestly seeking to know God, not for what I could *get,* but for the calm, peace, and joy of being in God's presence. I was being reminded of what I'd always believed, that my mind is powerful and that I co-create my life with God by what I focus on and how I think.

One of the phrases often repeated at Christ Universal Temple, where Johnnie pastored, was "Change your thinking, change your life." This part is crucial and probably the most opposed to what I'd been taught in church coming up. I learned that what happens in my life specifically relates to what I think and believe about myself, and my actions over the years indicated that I believed many lies. For instance, what I saw and experienced early in my life laid the groundwork for my belief that abuse in a relationship was okay, that lack was the norm, and that infidelity was to be expected. These weren't beliefs I held on a conscious level, but I came to understand that my subconscious mind is directing my experiences. I began to understand that one of the first steps in changing my beliefs was to change my thoughts. This would take work, but I was up for the challenge.

First, I had to recognize and admit the part I played in my experiences. A lot of that started when I began to believe the things that had happened to me *were* me. I had to look back and rebuke the voice that told me my father's incarceration equaled his abandonment of me. It didn't. Neither did his abuse and disrespect of our entire family mean that I was worthless or that anything he said to me from his hurting place was true about me. I had to forgive myself and acknowledge that the abuse and disrespect of my mind, body, and spirit by the predators who crossed my path was *their* sickness, but accepting the abuse again and again because of what I'd learned to believe about myself was up to me to stop.

Elevating my beliefs about myself and my worth didn't mean the predators would magically disappear, but it did empower me to recognize them and put up my "force field" against them.

Love yourself and you will be loved

Not long after I'd been going to Christ Universal Temple, my friend George introduced me to a friend of his. Tommy and I hit it off right away and soon he was joining me at church. He experienced the same "at home" feeling I did, and we joined the church together. Our relationship grew and after we'd been dating about two years, we were married by one of our class instructors, who was also on the church's ministerial staff. When we got married in October, my entire family came to help us celebrate. This time, my father was completely sober and he brought the two daughters he'd had since he and my mother separated. He'd finally recognized what a terror these girls' mother was and left her. He was healing and working to be a good dad to all of his children.

My mom, in her usual beautiful, forgiving way, had become friends again with my dad and they laughed and talked together like the past had all been a bad dream.

This isn't happening

Tommy and I excitedly planned our lives together. We both wanted children and had every belief that we'd be pregnant in no time. For a minute, all seemed right with the world. For a minute. Almost a year to the date of our first anniversary, in early October, Tommy started having really bad body aches. He'd come home from his job at FedEx, a job my beautiful Aunt Candy also helped to facilitate, saying his ribs, back, or neck hurt. When neither heat, nor ice, nor rest gave him any relief, he finally agreed to see a doctor. It turned out the pain in his ribs was because he'd cracked three of them, but even the doctors didn't readily know why.

We continued to go from one doctor to another, looking for the source of Tommy's pain. December 6 is the anniversary of the day I learned of my dear friend Rosena's transition. In 1996, it was also the day my daddy called to tell us he'd been diagnosed with lung cancer. I was stunned into silence! When I finally regained my voice, I vowed right then to fight with him and for him. Daddy quietly agreed that he could beat this and told me how much he loved and appreciated me before he hung up to call and break the news to other family members. I won't go into that entire conversation or journey now, but saying that I felt sucker-punched is an understatement.

After visiting many doctors, enduring countless tests and wrong guesses, five months later, in March of the following year, we finally got a correct diagnosis for what was causing Tommy's pain: multiple myeloma—cancer! The doctors told us they'd had such a difficult time diagnosing the disease because it's typically found in people decades older than my husband's forty-four years. Tommy had spent many years in asbestos abatement and I believe with all my heart that this was the cause of his death sentence. We sat in tearful disbelief as they told us he had about five years to live. I didn't know it at the time, but my daddy had been given a much grimmer report.

How could this be? The two men I loved most in the world were both facing terminal illnesses. I did my best to give my time and attention to both of them, but Daddy was in Rockford and I had a lot less say—or I believed I did—in his care than I did in my husband's.

They started Tommy on chemotherapy and the drug they used to keep him alive simultaneously killed our dreams of having biological children. The poison that is chemotherapy kills not only the cancer cells, but sperms cells, too. But we couldn't worry about that then. My only focus was defying the odds. Tommy and I immediately became vegans and later, raw foodists. I had him drinking wheatgrass juice and taking oxygen baths. I prepared food, joined him at his doctor's appointments, did my best to comfort him as he faced his fears, and did research on how to fight the Big C, all while working crazy long hours as a loan officer. I became a loan officer after being unceremoniously laid off after ten years at Xerox, six months after I bought the house Tommy moved into with me after we were married. Only six months after I made the serious commitment of homeownership, I was jobless! Now, *that* was interesting!

I couldn't see it at the time because I was so overwhelmed, but I now wish I'd brought Daddy on my healing quest right along with Tommy. I was in Rockford as much as possible and was constantly on the phone with my dad, but I wish we'd had more time—more time to heal and to ask more of my "why," "what," and "how" questions. But, like most of us, I thought we had more time than we did.

Call to Action: If we keep our hearts open, relationships can be healed. Yes, it takes work and forgiveness, but it is possible and so worth it!

Please see *Healing Waters: The Workbook* for resources, exercises, meditations, conversation starters, and more on how to rebuild broken relationships.

Chapter 20

This Can't Be Right! I'm Not Ready!

Please, Daddy, don't leave me again! Not yet! Please!

*I*n October of that year, ten months after Daddy was first diagnosed, he asked me to come to Rockford to be with him in the hospital while the doctors ran more tests. His cancer, which had miraculously gone into remission a few months earlier, was back and the doctors wanted to see exactly where it had metastasized to. When I got there, he gave me a big smile along with a laugh (that I can still hear!) and his usual greeting.

"Hey, Ang! How are you doing, honey?"

God, I love both of my parents so much! While my mom has never wavered in her unadulterated joy in seeing me, now my dad always showed the same excitement! That kind of unfiltered love and acceptance is what peace, good mental health, and lasting success are built on. Every child, every *person,* deserves it.

"I'm good, Daddy, but how are *you*?" I asked.

"I'm good, kiddo. Trusting that my tests come back better than they expect."

"Well, let's have a word of prayer before you go down and trust God for your healing."

After we shared a word of prayer, I walked next to his chair as they wheeled him down for the MRI.

Afterward, we sat in his room, chatting about everything and nothing as we waited for the results.

When the doctor appeared in the doorway, grim and quiet, we knew the news wasn't going to be good. He told us that my beloved daddy had, at best, a week to live.

Daddy and I left the hospital in shock that Thursday evening because the doctor told us the DNR order neither Daddy nor I agreed with was the best course to take. He told us resuscitation would only prolong the inevitable and cause my daddy unnecessary pain. We were both silent as we tried to absorb the notion that there was nothing more medical science could do and Daddy's transition was near. When we got to his house, for the first couple of hours it was just the two of us. We talked quietly about his fears; he really wasn't ready to make his transition. He still had so much he wanted to do. So much he wanted to say to me, the rest of his children, my mom, other family members, and some of his friends. He still felt like he had much to offer the world. He felt that he really hadn't had the opportunity to fully, freely, and happily live. He felt that there was so much he hadn't seen or experienced. He still knew that success and greatness lived within him and he wanted the chance to express it. We cried softly for a minute before he put on a brave face and made a joke about still being around to protect me, even if he wasn't in a body! Hmm, on second thought, that probably wasn't a joke. (I welcome your presence, Daddy! All day, any day, every day!)

Eventually, a few more family members showed up, teary-eyed and speechless. Around 10:00 p.m., I could tell Daddy was tired, so I asked those who weren't immediate family to let him get some rest. I made sure he was as comfortable in bed as possible. I checked his oxygen tank and the line to make sure all was flowing smoothly, then took the chair beside his bed to rest my eyes and my mind. A couple of hours later, I could hear Daddy moving around. I looked up and he was heading toward the door, pulling his oxygen tank.

"Where you going, Daddy?"

"Outside to get some fresh air. You wanna come?" For the end of October, it was unseasonably warm and the T-shirts we had on were all we needed to feel comfortable.

"Of course I'm coming with you," I replied.

When we got to the porch and took our seats, my daddy, lifelong smoker that he was, pulled out a cigarette!

"What are you doing?" I exclaimed.

"Ang, I think at this point it doesn't matter if I smoke or not. I might as well enjoy it." Our tear-filled eyes met and we exchanged a lifetime of conversations in those few moments. I squeezed his hand and sat next to him while we stared into the darkness and he smoked what would be one of his last cigarettes.

I was only in Rockford that Thursday to accompany Daddy to his doctor's appointment and I had planned to return to Chicago that evening. The unexpectedly devastating news kept me there overnight. On Friday I went back home to Chicago to pack a bag and check on my husband, who was feeling ill due to his own terminal cancer diagnosis and chemotherapy treatments. I'd planned to return to Rockford Sunday night, giving me enough time to prepare a few meals for Tommy and make sure he was good. That was my plan, but late Saturday morning I got a call from my mom telling me that I needed to head back right away. Things weren't looking good for Daddy to make it through the night. I threw a change of clothes in a bag and hugged my husband, who sent me off with a quick word of prayer and encouragement, and ran out the door. I've never driven so fast! I prayed for the police or state troopers to stop me so they could escort me through the traffic at even higher speeds, but they all must have been changing shifts because I sped along the expressway undeterred. I shaved twenty or thirty minutes off of the normal two-hour travel time from our door to my dad's.

There were a lot of cars parked at his house, so instead of looking for one farther away and having to walk back to his house, I drove right over the curb, the sidewalk, and his grass, pulling right up to the stairs. I'd barely put the car in park before I was jumping out and running into the house. I dropped my purse on the floor right inside the door (which turned out to be a big mistake since $200 was missing from it when I finally retrieved it although I was in a house full of "family and friends") and pushed my way through the crowd who'd gathered to see my daddy, comfort him, and pray for him.

151

"Daddy, I'm here!" I whispered in his ear as I held his hand.

He looked at me with that big grin that said, "I'm so glad, honey. I love you." Conditions can change in a heartbeat. In less than forty-eight hours, my daddy went from sitting on the porch, talking with me with relative strength and clarity, to not being able to talk at all. I wasn't ready! I still had questions! I still needed answers! We'd grown so much; our relationship had healed immensely over the previous twelve or so years, but I felt cheated! I still needed my daddy. I needed his hugs, his words of encouragement, his love! It seems that he knew it because he rallied. His condition stabilized and, again, we cleared the house of everyone but the closest friends and family.

Even though Daddy could no longer talk, he made eye contact and could nod, shake his head, or gesture with his hands when asked a question. He let us know that he wanted to be cleaned up. I asked him if he wanted a shave. He nodded and it was my honor to give him the last one of his time on this earth. I got a basin with warm water, towels, his razor, shaving cream, and aftershave and gratefully and gently applied the cream, then carefully shaved his face. He turned his head and lifted his chin as necessary to make it easier for me to give him a close shave. More than once when tears blurred my vision, I had to stop so I wouldn't cut him. For the second time in less than two days, we had an entire conversation with our eyes. I knew for sure that my daddy loved me, and in those moments all the pain, heartbreak, and disappointment that had filled my childhood dissolved into forgiveness, compassion, and longing for more time.

Devil in the form of an "ex"

Daddy's second ex-wife, the one who had done her level best to make life hell for my siblings, my mom and I, and later my dad, was there along with the two daughters she'd had when she was with my dad. Ex Two forced her way into the bedroom and insisted on being at his side. Every time she touched him, he cringed and squirmed. Why couldn't she see that she wasn't helping? That she was making him more uncomfortable than he already was? She eventually forced me out of the room, saying she wanted a few minutes of private time with him. I can still see the look of painful, pleading desperation in his eyes as she all but shoved me out the door. It sickens me to think what she might have said or done in the ten or fifteen minutes she had alone with him. I wish I'd stood my ground, honored Daddy's wishes, and made *her* leave!

On Sunday, Daddy was still doing okay; he was stable and drinking Ensure through a straw. Around two o'clock Monday morning, even though I'd had next to no sleep, I decided to dash back to Chicago and really pack a bag, thinking I'd be back later that afternoon. On the drive back, it began to snow heavily. It was pretty, but unsettling. Just three evenings earlier, Daddy and I had sat on his front porch in our T-shirts. It was only October 27, a little early for so much snow, I thought.

I was exhausted both physically and emotionally. I climbed into bed next to my husband around 4:30 a.m. It seemed I'd just closed my eyes when the ringing phone woke me up. I groggily answered to my mom's quiet cries.

"Your daddy's gone, honey," she said softly through her tears. It was just after seven.

"What?! No! That's impossible! I just left and he was doing okay! Please, Ma, tell me he's not gone!"

"I'm sorry, honey. He is. Get a little more sleep and come back home. We won't let them move him until you get here. I love you, sweetheart."

"I love you, too, Mommy. I'll be there as soon as I can." I lay there, sobbing. I was grieving so much at the loss of my daddy, the loss of what could have been, and the lingering unresolved pain that we continued to process. How could this be?

Tommy tried his best to comfort me, but I was inconsolable. I think, too, that he had to be thinking of his own mortality. Only seven months earlier, we'd sat in the doctor's office and listened to the news that he probably had no more than five years to live himself. How could that not be looming large in his mind?

After a while, I dragged myself out of bed and packed a bag while I called my older half-sister, Val, who also lived in Chicago, to tell her.

She asked me to pick her up and take her back to Rockford with me. I reluctantly agreed. Not because I didn't want her to be there or even that I didn't want to give her a ride—I wanted to be in Rockford *now* and picking her up would add at least ninety minutes to my trip. It turned out that it added over three hours to our trip because she wasn't ready when I arrived at her house.

When we got to Rockford, as my beautiful mom had promised, Daddy was still laying in his bed. After greeting my family, Val and I went in to say our goodbyes to our dad. My daddy always had a beautiful head of long, thick hair and enough time had passed since his last round of chemo that it was back. I got a pair of scissors and a baggie and cut some from the back of his head, where the missing hair wouldn't be noticed.

When we'd had some time with him both together and separately, my mom called the coroner, and the ambulance came and took his body to the funeral home owned by some people Deb knew.

The next day things really started to get interesting. The former step-monster, Ex Two, came back and brought her daughters with her. My mom, siblings including Val, and a couple of daddy's siblings announced that we were going to the funeral home to handle the arrangements. Daddy had insurance, but sadly, he hadn't taken care of his final arrangements. This put us in the unfortunate position of having to figure out how to pay for everything.

Ex Two exclaimed loudly in her typical unpleasant fashion, "If my girls can't go, we're not helping financially!"

We tried to explain to her that we weren't excluding them. We just felt that at their very young ages (they were preteens) the experience might be traumatic for them. She wasn't trying to hear that, though. She mumbled and groaned under her breath. We should have remembered that Daddy brought one of the devil's spawn into our lives, but we were too distracted to think about her.

My daddy loved model cars and he had an amazing collection! These cars were beautiful, all perfectly painted, with hoods, trunks, and doors that all opened. The interiors were immaculate. They were his pride and joy! We returned from our first visit to the funeral home to find that Ex Two and Daddy's youngest brother had removed every single car from his home. They didn't consider that the rest of us might want a memento to remember Daddy by. No, they selfishly took them all for themselves. Ex Two had also run to the Social Security Administration with falsified documents to claim the $225 given to the families of each American who transitions.

Clearly, she didn't love my daddy and was too evil and committed to plotting and planning to shed a tear of grief and loss. I wish I could say that things stopped there, but that would be too boring! No, while we were gone, not only did she have time to engage in thievery, but she also took the time to incite her girls. We were only back a short time before they started screaming and crying, saying we "never liked them" and we were horrible for "not wanting them to be included in Daddy's funeral arrangements." The oldest daughter was the most vocal. She yelled in our faces that she hated us and thought we were awful. We tried to explain that we had absolutely no ill feelings toward them, that they were children and we'd never had an issue with them. What I thought but didn't say was, It's your deceitful momma that we can't stand. We don't hold her whorish, evil ways against *you*. Don't believe her lies. It seems her big goal in life is to sow seeds of dissension wherever she goes.

Somehow, we made it through the services without throwing hands. All six of us—Mommy's three, Val, and the other two Daddy claimed—even got close enough to take a group picture together.

Sadly, Daddy delivered one last soul blow from the grave. He made Val, the step-monster, and the other two girls beneficiaries of his insurance policy, while leaving his first and forever family the bill for his final arrangements. Some of Daddy's siblings helped us out and for that we are grateful. Although Val promised to contribute, she never gave one dime. Nothing was expected from the other two or their mom and we weren't disappointed. Soon after the services, all communication stopped between the three of us and the three of them. While I wish each of them well, I honestly can't say that it matters. Daddy was the only glue that bound us and I guess now we don't have to pretend.

Some years before Daddy's transition, he took the other three girls to spend time with his siblings and their families. Deb, Dean, and I were routinely excluded from these family gatherings. This, along with being left out as beneficiaries of Daddy's life insurance policy, bothered me for years. One day it all clicked into place: first, the four of us—me, Mom, and my siblings—reminded Daddy of his ugliest parts. The other three allowed the illusion of a clean slate and didn't evoke a constant need to apologize, explain, or make amends. He could more easily "stand up inside himself" with them.

Second, all our lives, our mom exhibited extraordinary strength in being able to weather any storm Daddy created with grace and relative financial stability, not as an affront to him or his manhood, but because that's how she's made. Instead of making excuses, all she knows, all she's ever done, is make a way out of no way. Her three children learned and live this same strength. I believe Daddy felt that we never really needed him. Oh, he was so wrong. We may not have necessarily needed him financially, but we desperately needed his love, support, encouragement, and mental and emotional stability. To paraphrase Jill Scott again, we could do all these things by our damn selves, but we *needed* him! Withholding his presence in life and his finances in death was misguided and spoke to his feelings of unworthiness. Yes, it was painful, but I "get" him now.

> **Call to Action:** Please handle your business as it relates to your final affairs. This includes having and maintaining life insurance so your family doesn't need to ask for donations to "put you away."

Please see *Healing Waters: The Workbook* for many more suggestions and resources that can help you prepare for the inevitable.

Chapter 21

Is That Sunshine?!

◆————————•————————◆

"Faith is packing the sunscreen lotion in the midst of the storm."
Angel Allen Townsend

ommy lived twelve years, seven years longer than the doctors had predicted. Even though we eventually separated for hard and sad reasons I choose not to share in this book, he was a bright light in my life and I am honored to have been his wife. I've stopped asking myself why we had such a short and challenging time together. I choose to appreciate the unconditional love and the friendship we shared from the day we met until the day he took his last breath.

I also had to forgive myself and learn to love me—all of me. As I got better at loving myself, the universe honored me with a new opportunity to give and receive healthy love. I believe that coincidences are so much more than chance. As I scrolled through my phone to find the number of a business associate that I called all the time, *this* time my eyes landed on Shababa's name and number. Shababa, whose name differs by one letter from my business associate, was a great guy whom I'd gotten to know years earlier when we both visited our mutual friends. I knew him to be kind, intelligent, thoughtful and funny. We were both married at the time, but Tommy didn't join me when I visited these friends and I never met his then-wife. It didn't matter; we were part of a group of friends and nothing else. We, along with our mutual friends, enjoyed many delicious meals and lively conversations, but when our friends moved to California, we didn't stay in touch.

Before I'd given it a second thought, I clicked on his name thinking I'd just say hello after years of not talking to him. He answered and during our chat, we found that we were both single and agreed to meet for lunch.

That "chance" phone call to say hello to an old acquaintance led to many more conversations, a true friendship, exclusive dating, world travel and eventually our loving marriage that is almost a decade strong.

I attribute the blessing of marrying men that I call "friend" to consciously directing my thinking in ways that promote healing, joy and love. This thinking, this way of being, was modeled by my mother my entire life. Going to Christ Universal Temple helped me to put "meat on those bones." Wanting to understand the way the mind works eventually led me to study and become a consulting hypnotist (CH). I could not have asked for a better Certification Instructor! Even now, years after I became certified, Linda Williamson remains on my speed dial list. She happily welcomes my calls and shares a process or tidbit of important information that never fails to further enlighten me or get me right back on track. I learned through hypnosis how to access the subconscious mind to replace thoughts that produced negative behaviors and outcomes with thoughts that could help me and others create the lives we want. Then, many years ago when I was looking for a therapist, my dear friend Jocelyn introduced me to her cousin Atara. Dr. Atara not only became my longtime therapist, but has become a mentor, one of my cheerleaders, my go-to metaphysician, and a fellow CH. When I forget my role in my movie, get stuck in my "stuff," or want to have a pity party about what's been "done to me," Linda, Jocelyn or Atara is right there to remind me of my power and my responsibility to do the work to stay awake and live my life with honesty, purpose, and clarity.

I wish I could say I never stumbled again, but the truth is that the work doesn't end. The fight continues. Thinking that life is unfair or that it shouldn't be this hard doesn't make the enemy (within) of love, joy, peace, and success give me a timeout. The predators still show up. They sometimes get harder to recognize, though. I experienced one or two more abusive relationships before I met my loving husband Shababa. Now I work to have an open mind when I meet new people, but I keep my eyes wide open as well. I pay close attention to a new person's words *and* actions as they relate both to me and to others.

What I know now is that I must always respect and nurture the two most important relationships I could ever have: my relationship with God and my relationship with myself. When things seemed good and I spent more time enjoying the "fat of the land" and less time in quiet reflection, prayer, and study, I was completely caught off guard and unprepared to respond when something fell apart.

I also found roller skating, which brings me a joy that is almost indescribable! Of course, it doesn't take the place of my relationships with God, my husband, family, or friends, but it satisfies, exhilarates, and calms me all at the same time. When I've been profoundly sad, skating has helped me release endorphins that bring the sunshine out again. I'm always learning something new—a new move or something about myself and how I learn, stick with things or approach things. It's physical *and* relaxing. I've met a lot of beautiful people at the skating rinks, some who have become good friends. Skaters really are, in many ways, a family. It's hard not to be when you see the same people who love a sport as much as you do every week for years or even decades. I really do see skating as another one of God's many gifts to me and I plan to roll until the wheels fall off!

"Stay ready so you don't have to get ready." Will Smith

Another maxim I often heard Johnnie use was "The greatest cause of suffering is forgetfulness." I've forgotten that phrase and its importance more than once. At times, I have forgotten that the foundation of my life is God and that staying close *is* my peace. I have forgotten that the fight against my peace, joy, and health is ferocious and that I have to be diligent in fighting back. I have forgotten that I have to protect my mind from crazy thoughts about not being deserving or good enough. I have to remind myself regularly of the truth: That I am *"fearfully and wonderfully made"* (Psalm 139:14). That "I am the thinker who thinks the thought that makes the thing." I have to remember to slow down and pay attention to everything that's going on around me, to listen closely to what people say *and* don't say. I've said for many years, "What you do shouts so loud that I can't hear what you say." Now, I live by that truth. I've learned to watch what people do, how they act and react, both when they know they're being watched and when they don't.

I remind myself of the importance of being my best self in every way, while at the same time engaging in loving and forgiving self-care. I now guard my space, time, and energy zealously. I know that "No" is a complete sentence that requires no explanation or apology. There was a time when I'd sell myself short and play down my knowledge and experience. I now recognize and appreciate that I've done a lot of work to find my peace and I have an overflowing tool bag to get me back on track and keep me moving in the right direction.

It took me a long time to get here, but I am finally okay with my truth, all of it. I'm so okay with it that I invest very little energy in what others might think of me and my life, then or now. This doesn't make me arrogant; it's just the opposite. It makes me humble, human, and, I hope, brave. I know we all have warts, bruises, and experiences we might want to forget, as does anyone who might try to judge me and mine. I pray and believe that by sharing my experiences, I can help others feel less alone and find hope that healing and triumph over their trials is possible. The pain, fear, and embarrassment I endured for years has morphed into excitement—excitement that my story, the beautiful thread of God's grace that has been woven throughout, and the strength I found to fight my way out might serve to help light the way, even just a little, for individuals, families, and communities impacted by incarceration, rape, homelessness, abuse, and other violent interruptions.

Call to Action: Give yourself permission to love you! Give yourself permission to accept your truth. Give yourself permission to make mistakes, to grow, to love, and to accept love. Give yourself permission to have fun!

Please see *Healing Waters: The Workbook* for exercises, resources, meditations, and more ways to support your journey to self-acceptance.

Epilogue

*A*s I mentioned earlier, my father got sober and spent years rebuilding relationships with me, my sister and brother, *and* my mom! We shared countless conversations about living healthy, happy, and fulfilling lives. We read books together, traveled together, and built businesses together. He and my mom developed a strong and solid friendship and she was at his side when he succumbed to lung cancer at the far-too-young age of fifty-eight. She never stopped loving him and today, over twenty years after his transition, she still does.

Our beautiful mom, who first showed me how to fight, is fighting still. Her grit, focus, humor, faith in God, and light continue to inspire everyone she meets. Being near her and hearing her voice and musical laughter, as well as seeing her gorgeous smile that can brighten a day, a room, and a mood, all make *my* day. I thank my God for making her my mom and blessing me with her love, support, and friendship. I strive daily to be at least half as forgiving, loving, joyful, kind and optimistic as she is naturally. My siblings and I agree that her example makes us stronger, kinder, and more compassionate and patient. We remain extremely close and enthusiastically draw our spouses, families, and friends into the orbit of love she ignites in each of us.

My brother is an amazing man and my friend. He selflessly pours into our mom as she takes on yet another major fight, this one for her health. Every day, he exudes a level of kindness, patience, courage, and strength that I believe surprises even him. I am forever grateful for his unending commitment. We consciously work on our relationship and our communication skills. We are both committed to making our friendship the best it can be.

My sister, a beautiful soul and yes, my dear friend too, has a loving husband and two great children. She and I remain committed to our friendship and make dates to spend time together often. She's like sunshine, sharing a kind word, love, and light with everyone she meets. With grace, ease, and reverence, she handles the responsibility of ministry that God has entrusted her with, delivering teachings that help people to live free and healthy lives.

My Aunt Elois and I remained close over the years. My mom traveled with her and her family. Our families enjoyed countless events together and she remained a confidant until, sadly, she began a battle with dementia that she succumbed to in 2016.

Even though my Aunt Candy moved to another state to be closer to her daughter, son-in-law, and grandchildren, we still talk often and she remains my friend, confidant, sounding board, prayer partner, cheerleader, and advisor. She's been a calm and steady force in my life and I am forever grateful for her love and guidance.

Charlotte is a sweetheart and is living a golden life. She's the proud mom and grandmother to several children and grandchildren. She has a quick, easy laugh and a positive attitude. While the busyness of life keeps us from talking as often as we'd like, when we do, we effortlessly pick up right where we left off. She is and will always be my sister-friend.

Sheila, my childhood friend, my first college roommate, and Triple G (Good, Good Girlfriend!), and I are still making fun memories together. We support and work with each other in business. We pray with and for each other and we travel together. I am eternally grateful to have her as a lifelong friend who's seen me morph from a caterpillar to a butterfly and has loved and accepted me unconditionally every step of the way!

Lynn suddenly made her transition while I was writing this book and we weren't able to completely mend our relationship. Even though I didn't share a lot in this book about the good parts of our relationship, there were some, and while we didn't talk as much in later years, I know, at one point, we had love for each other. I choose to honor our good and pray for her peaceful rest.

Last, but certainly not least, is my blessing, my husband, Shababa. Shababa is calm when I am sometimes storm. I first met him when I wasn't ready for him, still floundering and hurting. He reappeared years later when we were both ready and available. He's fine, kind, thoughtful, loving, giving, steady, stable and fun! He loves the Lord, and he prays with, for and over me. As with any relationship, it's not always easy, but we are committed to growing, ever learning and evolving together. He is truly a godsend. Thank You, Father God, for the hook-up!

My church and spiritual life have continued to evolve as well. My husband is a member and deacon at Trinity United Church of Christ, and I am now a proud and active member, too. I'm excited and honored to be a part of a village that is "Unashamedly Black and Unapologetically Christian"! Our pastor, the Reverend Dr. Otis Moss III, and his lovely wife, First Lady Monica, helm a church that is absolutely perfect for where I am today as a growing, healing Woman of God. The teaching there supports my ever-deepening and evolving relationship with God, myself, my husband, my family and my community. Our favorite parts of the week are being in church on Sundays and many Wednesdays.

When I first published this book, I wrote about my memories and experiences with two relatives from a place of unresolved hurt and disappointment. Growth and God's grace led to healing and understanding. If you're reading this, your copy includes changes that don't alter the truth but highlight the biggest picture: that Love and True Peace really are possible through forgiveness and acceptance. We can having the healing or we can stick to the "story" of pain, heartache and disappointment, but we can't have both. I choose healing. I hope you will, too.

End Notes

Chapter 2

- Black men sentenced to more time for committing the exact same crimes as a white person, study finds. By Christopher Ingraham, 11-06-2017

- Racial Disparity in Criminal Sentences, 2014, University of Michigan Law School Scholarship Repository. https://repository.law.umich.edu/articles/1414

- Demographic Differences In Sentencing: An Update to the 2012 Booker Report, United States Sentencing Commission, November, 2017

Chapter 3

- Can trauma be passed down from one generation to the next? Karina Marit Erdelyi. https://www.psycom.net/epigenetics-trauma

- What is generational trauma? Here's how experts explain it. Claire Gillespie Health.com 10/2020

- Legacy of trauma: Context of the African American existence. By Brandon Jones, M.A., Psychotherapist & Behavioral Health Consultant

- The curse of slavery has left an intergenerational legacy of trauma and poor health for African Americans, Michael J Halloran

- Parents' emotional trauma may change their children's biology, ScienceMag.org, Andrew Curry, July 18, 2019

Chapter 6

- https://www.ucg.org/the-good-news/a-generation-of-abandonment

- https://www.goodtherapy.org/learn-about-therapy/issues/ abandonment#:~:text=Abandonment%20fears%20can%20impair%20 a,(BPD)%20and%20attachment%20anxiety.

Chapter 8

- BullyingStatistics.org
  Anti-Bullying Help, Facts and More
  Bullying and Suicide

- CDC.gov
  The Relationship Between Bullying and Suicide
  National Center for Injury Prevention and Control
  Division of Violence Prevention

- VeryWellFamily
  8 Reasons Why Teens Bully Others, October 11, 2020
  Sherri Gordon

Chapter 12

- SentencingProject.org

Locked Out 2020
Estimates of People Denied Voting Rights Due to A Felony
Conviction

Chapter 17

* National Institute of Mental Health
  Nimh.nih.gov/health/statistics/suicide.shtml

* Associates for Women's Medicine
  Warning Signs of Suicide
  Current as of September 23, 2020

Notes

_____

_____

_____

_____

_____

_____

_____

_____

_____

_____

_____

_____

Notes

Notes